W9-CHF-120

PENGUIN BOOKS

LOOKING BEYOND THE IVY LEAGUE
Finding the College That's Right for You

Loren Pope first started writing about education with a column for the Gannett Newspapers in 1952, which led to the education editorship of *The New York Times* during the height of the college-going chaos of the late fifties. Then, and later as a top administrator of what is now Oakland University in Michigan, he was deeply concerned with the lack of consumer information on colleges; the uninformed way in which most families chose colleges; and the heavy dropout, transfer, and failure rate that resulted.

In 1965, he opened the College Placement Bureau in Washington to help families make informed, fruitful choices. Out of his reporting and research came a book, *The Right College: How to Get In, Stay In, Get Back In* (Macmillan, 1970), and several magazine articles, including the nationally syndicated "Twenty Myths That Can Jinx Your College Choice," first published in *The Washington Post Magazine. Reader's Digest* has sold half a million reprints of its condensation, titled "Facts to Know in Picking a College."

Pope has been a contributor to professional journals and a speaker at meetings of the National Association of College Admissions Counselors. He has also appeared on radio and television.

LOOKING

Beyond

THE

Ivy League

FINDING THE COLLEGE THAT'S RIGHT FOR YOU

Loren Pope

Penguin Books

PENGUIN BOOKS
Published by the Penguin Group
Viking Penguin, a division of Penguin Books USA Inc.,
375 Hudson Street, New York, New York 10014, U.S.A.
Penguin Books Ltd, 27 Wrights Lane,
London W8 5TZ, England
Penguin Books Australia Ltd, Ringwood,
Victoria, Australia
Penguin Books Canada Ltd, 10 Alcorn Avenue, Suite 300,
Toronto, Ontario, Canada M4V 3B2
Penguin Books (N.Z.) Ltd, 182-190 Wairau Road,
Auckland 10, New Zealand

Penguin Books Ltd, Registered Offices:
Harmondsworth, Middlesex, England

First published in Penguin Books 1990

10 9 8 7 6 5 4

LIBRARY OF CONGRESS CATALOGING IN PUBLICATION DATA
Pope, Loren.
Looking beyond the Ivy League : finding the college that's right
for you / Loren Pope.
    p.   cm.
ISBN 0 14 01.2209 5
1. College, Choice of—United States.   2. Universities and
colleges—United States—Evaluation.   I. Title.
LB2350.5.P67   1990
378.1′056′0973 — dc20   89–38784

Printed in the United States of America
Set in Cheltenham Light
Designed by Ann Gold

Behind every good man there's a good woman.

—My friend Jane B.

In my case it took three:

Ann Garman Rittenberg, vice president of the Julian Bach Literary Agency and former client (good small college), who made me shape this up so she could market it

Viola, who denies being a sharp reader of copy

And Lori Lipsky of Viking Penguin, whose incisive editing and on-the-mark suggestions sharpened and brightened the message

Acknowledgments

Aside from their contributions to this book, I am indebted to those named and many not named for the pleasure of having worked with them. Those who have been kind enough to let me use their personal statements and essays are Laura Banfield, Amherst '91; Susan Beal, Antioch '92; Andrew Butterfield, Oberlin '83; Morton Lapides, American U. '88; Josie McQuail, Virginia '78; Aviva Mirels, Washington U. '91; Robert Nieweg, Vassar '83; Jeff Ressin, Rensselaer '86; Robert Rogers, William and Mary '90; Kate Rourke, Yale '90; Elizabeth Tobias, Hamilton '89; Jim Whitaker, Georgetown '90. Also, Virginia Wright, Johns Hopkins '87, who as a graduate fellow at Columbia counseled me on Chaucer, among other things.

Among those who testified to the effects of their undergraduate experiences were Margaret Carroll, the Rev. Pinckney Ennis, Stephanie Flathman, L. Jo Froman, and Edith Uunila Taylor. I am indebted to Claire Matthews of Connecticut College, Jim White of Oberlin, and Jim Baer of Wabash for their views and help on financial aid, and to *The Chronicle of Higher Education* for the several quotations from it, and especially for permission to reprint the article by Sam Bittner. Also to *The Washington*

Post for permission to reprint "Twenty Myths That Can Jinx Your College Choice," and to the *Oberlin Review* for permitting me to reprint "A Place to Come To." Penelope Hadley, Elizabeth and Virginia Wright, and Anna Horsbru-Porter spent many hours combing through the biographies in *Who's Who in America* to find out where those listed went to college.

Contents

Introduction

This book of mine, which will help fulfill your college command "Open Sesame!" is a lot more than a magic phrase. It brings an unmatched expertise—thirty-five years of investigating and writing about colleges, of being a college official, and of counseling students and their parents on good educational goals—to help you open the door of the right college.

Opening your Sesame may not be done easily, much less with a single command, but the enlightenment and guidance herein will not only give you confidence in the task but make it rewarding for a lifetime.

Long ago, I was frustrated as a parent to find out that while there was plenty of objective data, there were few guiding clues for picking suitable colleges, a feeling later reinforced when I became a writer on education. As college-going had surged from 10 percent before World War II to over 50 percent, the quest had become a public frenzy. The criteria most people used—and still use—such as name and prestige, have regularly and consistently failed the test: when I started an education column for the Gannett Newspapers in 1952, only 40 percent of the freshmen were in the same colleges after four years. The most recent study found that the percentage had shrunk to a third.

Later, as education editor of *The New York Times* at the crest of the hysteria, and as a top administrator of what is now Oakland University in Michigan, I developed a plan for consumer research on colleges to help people make more fruitful choices by providing the vital information the directories didn't and don't give. So I opened College Placement Bureau in 1965 to counsel kids and their parents and to help them choose colleges most likely to have a beneficial impact.

I discover the parents' backgrounds, where they went to college and why, what their original majors were and what they do now—usually no connection—and whether and when there's been a divorce that has hurt the child's grades. In long interviews with the student, whose academic records and writing samples are in hand, I get his history, interests, what he thinks his abilities and interests are, and his parents' reactions. With the parents out of the room, a lot of personal and Fifth Amendment questions elicit answers that help establish an understanding and give me a handle on him, what he values, and what he wants out of life. All this naturally reveals things that make it easier to help him say what he wants to say about himself in his personal statement and essay. It also enables me to discuss him more intelligently with an admissions officer.

With parents present, we talk about making high school part of the education, not just a stepping-stone, about reading, how to study, how to make Ralph Nader–type visits to test the college merchandise, how to make enlightened decisions, and about what college can and cannot do for the student. My concern is for the development of a unique individual. He may go to a name college, but that's not my test of success. Indeed, my college visits and researches have often shown well-known colleges to be inferior to little-known ones.

I have been able to show a family, for example, that going to a college they've never heard of will not only enhance the student's chances of getting into graduate school but may also do a more effective job of developing brains and character. And if the student is a girl, providing good female role models may give her more confidence to achieve.

The sum of my experience has kept me firmly in the company of the best minds in education who have always said that the small college, dedicated to a liberal education, is not just the wisest and most sensible, but the most practical. In a world in which most of tomorrow's jobs don't even exist yet, it is the only way, the truth, and the life. Today, even the specialists are being made converts; the people who hire them are seeing the light.

The future physicians, artists, newspapermen, or engineers can specialize later, after they've had some exposure to ideas that will make them better specialists and more versatile too, but first they must realize they are human beings, as John Donne said, involved in mankind. Graduate and professional schools don't liberate; they only turn out journeymen for diverse intellectual, legal, or commercial trades.

When Thomas Jefferson, himself the founder of a university, said there cannot be a democracy without an educated public, he meant an informed, moral, and enlightened public, not just a vocationally or professionally trained one. Today, with shamefully few exceptions, the universities have no such mission as producing informed, moral, and enlightened citizens. That role has been almost wholly assumed by the good liberal arts college.

The universities cheat the undergraduates and society because their values are antithetical to liberal education, and have been increasingly so ever since the post-World-War-II higher education boom. Sputnik, with its spending fever on math, science, and languages, made the universities primarily research businesses as they grew bigger and ever more impersonal. Now they serve the Mammon that provides them with building funds, research grants, and the prestige derived from research and publication. The tuition they get from undergraduates is pin money. For example, Johns Hopkins, with an enrollment of thirty-one hundred, gets about $37 million a year in tuition, but rakes in over $200 million in research money and $353 million in defense contracts. You don't have to be a churchgoer to know that where thy treasure is, there will thy heart be also.

These figures tell you why the universities relegate under-graduate education to second- or third-class status, and why they have made it a mass-production, assembly-line, career-oriented factory, and why that factory is largely manned by academic apprentices and serfs. The scholars have little or no contact with the students, yet socially ambitious and insecure parents and their children think the university with its famous scholars, its impressive physical facilities, its size, and its rep-utation will confer status and the assurance of a good future. Ironically, those same scholars were largely produced by the good small colleges the families ignore.

The good liberal arts college, the place where Jefferson's ideal is being realized, seeks to develop the reasonable and sensible men and women essential to a free society. In so doing, it also produces people who are more likely to enjoy fulfilling and productive lives, which makes it a better individual in-vestment as well.

The central message of this book is that while most college choices are so foolishly made that most students eventually forsake or flunk out of them, the best buyer's market in history offers almost any youth an array of colleges to choose from that can make a lifelong difference. And prestige has very little to do with it. What counts is the quality of the experience in developing the potential of the young person into the power of the mature adult, not the label. Furthermore, a lot of these colleges, far from turning down most of their applicants, want to be found. They are looking for you.

What I hope this book will do is to free parents and their sons and daughters from the worship of the false gods of name and size and prestige and help them identify the real virtues of

mental and moral growth, so they can make their most important investment, one that will give a lifetime of satisfaction. I
think I have clearly marked the path through the thicket of
irrelevancies, the perils, and the tempting snares to the castle
atop the hill. The reader can set out with confidence.

LOOKING BEYOND
THE IVY LEAGUE

1 🙠
Twenty Myths
That Can Jinx
Your College Choice

Year After Year After Year, They Go on Jinxing.

A house may be the costliest thing most families buy, but college—which is second—is far more important, because that investment affects their teenager's future. The four college years are the last important developmental period of youth, and what happens then has substantial, lifelong consequences. The youth can be awakened to develop himself and his talents. Or he can plod through largely untouched and unenlightened, bored and frustrated, leading him to transfer, drop out, or flunk out. Unbelievable as it may seem, nearly 70 percent of all students suffer one of these unhappy fates.

Even aside from such considerations as the credentials and the fun and status of going to college, the quality of the experience can make such a difference in a person's life that where he goes is more important than whether he goes. (He *could* educate himself on his own in the library.) The magic is in the moral and intellectual torque the college exerts, not in the name, however hallowed it may be. And a continuing irony of the annual college search is that in our vastly overbuilt education establishment so many good colleges are eager to be found that it is a buyer's market of first-rate academic bargains.

But how do intelligent parents and students, confronted with an array of two thousand possible choices, mostly shoddy or unsuitable, arrive at their decisions in making this critical and costly purchase? Do they do some probing consumer research? Do they ask for performance data? Do they sample and test the merchandise? No. And unfortunately there is no consumer research available to the public in this vital field. The reports of accrediting teams are more jealously guarded than any defense secret. There is much objective data in directories but few guiding clues to reveal the many obvious or subtle differences in ambience, values, or character among colleges of the same level of rigor, and none on the long-term performance of their products. No one would pick a wife or a husband or even buy a house or a car with so little information.

The result is that the American family relies chiefly on the pig-in-a-poke method of college selection, based on twenty myths that profoundly influence millions of unfortunate, and some fortunate, college choices. On the whole it is such bad consumerism that only 30 to 40 percent of any fall's freshman class will still be in the same colleges four years later. These myths constitute a body of dogma accepted as gospel by the able and mediocre student alike. Here they are, with the lowdown on each.

Myth One: An Ivy or Little Ivy College Will
Absolutely Guarantee the Rich, Full, and Successful Life.*

Five years out of college—and usually a lot sooner—a person's own qualities will be deciding whether he gets a raise, a promotion, is courted for another job, or has the vision to see new

---

* The eight universities constituting the Ivy League are Brown, Columbia, Cornell, Dartmouth (which calls itself a college), Harvard, Pennsylvania, Princeton, and Yale. The Little Ivies are Amherst, Wesleyan, and Williams.

opportunities and the imagination to create a new career. Even if the name on his diploma helped get the first job because it was taken as evidence of his intelligence, that would be about the limit of its leverage because most people change jobs at least once in the first five years. A young Princeton graduate, who had also been a National Merit Scholar, said: "Its value lasts about fifteen minutes." If the Ivies were as puissant as they are fashionable their graduates should have a stranglehold on all the honors lists and positions of power, especially since the Ivies have their pick of the country's best academic performers. But they don't; a disproportionate share of the honors has always been taken by little-known colleges. As Chapter 8 will show you, a search of *Who's Who in America* reveals that these schools contribute more than their share of the entries.

Myth Two: If You Can't Make an Ivy, a Prestige College
Is Next Best Because the Name on Your Diploma
Will Determine Whether You Get into a Good
Graduate School or Do Something Worthwhile in Life.

You can't get into any medical school with a C+ average from any name school, but you can with a B+ average and good Medical College Aptitude Test scores from Earlham or Knox or a host of other good schools. What counts is your record and your abilities. Furthermore, the graduate department chairman and some of the admissions committee members are as likely as not to be graduates of little freshwater colleges.

Myth Three: Eastern Institutions Are the Best and Most
Desirable; Southern Schools the Least Desirable;
and Forget About That Dreary Siberian Plain Between
Pennsylvania and the Colorado Ski Slopes
Known as the Midwest.

The Midwest has long been a victim of Eastern cultural prejudice; the South suffers a lingering damnation for sins of the past. The truth is quite different. The Midwest has a century-and-a-half tradition of easy access to quality higher education, both public and private, to which most of the East is a recent convert. Using the American Council on Education's ratings of graduate programs, made by graduate deans and six thousand scholars, all eight of the greatest public universities, except California, are in the Midwest. When Britain and Canada expanded higher education after World War II, their principal sources of ideas were not the Ivy League but the Midwestern universities.

Midwestern undergraduate colleges have been responsible for most of the innovations of recent years. The Common Application now used by one hundred colleges was originated twenty years ago by the Associated Colleges of the Midwest (ACM) and enabled a youth to apply with one application and one fee to any three colleges of the twelve in ACM. Such things as self-designed programs, a strong student voice in college governance, and all kinds of first-rate co-operative off-campus study programs, both foreign and domestic, are old hat in the Midwest.

Student bodies in many Midwestern colleges are more cosmopolitan and diversified than in many Eastern ones. For example, only 5 percent of Antioch's students come from Ohio. No college has more diversity than Oberlin. About 29 percent of Beloit's and Grinnell's students are Jewish, which bespeaks two things about a school outside the East: high quality and diversity. Why? Jews, who account for only about 3 percent of the population, yield to no group in their concern for good education and so are less constrained by East or West Coast provincialism. At Earlham, a Quaker school, over half the students come from more than five hundred miles away, and some years the freshman class has more Jews than Quakers, as well as more Catholics or Methodists.

The same could also be said about several colleges in the South. When black students were segregating themselves on many Northern campuses several years ago, I found blacks sprinkled throughout the dining rooms of several Southern colleges and they told me that socially the campuses were single communities, not separate ones.

In short, quality and diversity are distributed institutionally, not geographically. The chances of getting the best quality for a given grade point average are far better outside the crowded East, where second- and even third-rate colleges are even selective. As for attractive landscape, anyone parachuted without a clue onto any one of a hundred or more Midwest or Southern campuses would probably never guess what state he was in.

Myth Four: A Big University Offers a Broader, Richer Undergraduate Experience with Better Teaching, Wider Course Selection, and a More Diverse Student Body Than a College.

Quite the opposite: the university by its very nature cheats most undergraduates out of essential parts of their educational birthright. The university is primarily interested in research, publishing, consulting, and graduate teaching. For the professors, that's where the rewards are, not for teaching undergraduates, who are a by-product or a nuisance and are second-class citizens. Even some of the greatest universities leave over 70 percent of the freshman and sophomore instruction to graduate assistants, or worse, to foreigners who can barely speak English.

The university's oft-cited claim that having many fine research scholars affects the quality of undergraduate teaching is a false position that has misled the public too long. If the great scholar teaches undergraduates at all—and most teach few or none—he is likely to be only an animated book or a television performer in a big lecture hall. Furthermore, he's a middle man; all the great ideas are in the library where he got them. The student is short changed because he is only a passive ear when he should be a participant. Seldom does he have the opportunity for a continuing conversation with his teachers, one of the requisites of a good experience.

At a large university, one's grade for a term may depend on one or two multiple-choice exams. It may be nearly impossible to get help in some departments, and big university attrition rates run as high as 80 percent in four years. The vast array of 3,000 courses a university may boast is, for most students, illusory. After one meets the requirements for a major and the barest framework of a liberal education—which any good college provides—there's not much room left for most of the other 2,970. Further, as many a disillusioned student has said, "Try to get in one; they're all filled." Greater depth or breadth may be had by way of independent study or research in a smaller college.

Here is some firsthand testimony that points up the stark contrast:

Dr. Parker Marden, who went to Bates College and got his Ph.D. from Brown, left the faculty at Cornell University (enrollment eighteen thousand) to head a new sociology program at Lawrence University in Wisconsin (enrollment thirteen hundred). After a year he wrote:

> I would contend that in a reasonable comparison of their faculties, the advantage rests with Lawrence, not with the major university I know best or others with which I am acquainted. At the very least, Lawrence fulfills its announced mission in undergraduate education while claiming little else, while the major universities meet many obligations while failing to meet the one about which they are most vocal: the teaching of undergraduates.

The small size of the college community, he added, leads to greater visibility of the faculty and quick identification of incompetence, while at the big university anonymity hides inability.

Teaching at Lawrence, he said, is much harder, yet more persons do it well. For one thing, faculty have to be far more responsible for the student's education; they have close contact with the student and help him with his problems. At the big university faculty hide from the students or refer them to graduate assistants. Faculty members are also more responsible for their disciplines; they have to teach students who have a broader, less career-oriented outlook and most of whom are majoring in other fields. Consequently, Dr. Marden said, at Lawrence they have "a built-in crap detector."

"In my first term," he concluded, "I heard names that had been unmentioned in my presence since I left college: Plato, Swift, Emerson, Adam Smith, and others that I now recall to be rather central to a Western intellectual tradition."

Myth Five: A College You've Heard About Is Better, or at least Safer, Than One You Haven't.

This is one of the worst traps of all. The parents' knowledge is minimal; even the colleges they attended may not be the same institutions they were then. Guidance counselors don't have the time or the funds to do on-site investigation of colleges. College presidents' knowledge of other institutions is not just limited, it is insular.

Pay no attention to published ratings by college presidents. Most of them aren't educators; they're upwardly mobile executives looking for a cushy or prestigious foundation, corporation, or university spot. Few of them have any sense of mission. As one of the good ones told me once, "I never hear any discussion of educational matters at presidents' meetings." But they much admire an entrepreneur like the one who has made George Mason University in Virginia a booming commuter institution. Once an admissions director friend, griping about the nature of his president's concerns, said, "I read *The New York Times;* he reads *The Wall Street Journal.*"

At dinner one night a president was saying what a great job his friend was doing at Drew University and what a good school it was. I had spent a day there a few weeks earlier and found the library virtually empty three times in one day, but the pinball machines and such in the student union were doing an SRO business. And five of six faculty members, when asked what percentage of the students they came in contact with were serious about learning, said, "Oh, about five percent." A studio art teacher, whose class requires no studying or papers, said, "Most of them."

There are no ratings of undergraduate colleges as there are of graduate programs, and a first-rate college doesn't get its name in the newspapers simply because it has an impact on a young mind and heart. The reaction of parents and students to such a place often is, "I never heard of it." But if the name is familiar because the school buys athletes and wins games, it is often more acceptable. When Jacksonville University's basketball team broke into the big time a decade ago, admissions applications soared, but for the student it was not a whit better than the year before.

Myth Six: What Your Friends Say
About a College Is a Good Indicator.

This is the feeblest reason of all. It is the everybody-likes-vanilla rationale; they don't. It reflects the adolescent need for peer approval. Even if high school juniors and seniors did know anything about colleges, the catch would be that unless all of them had similar values, abilities, interests, and personal qualities, a lot of mismatches would occur.

Similarly, choosing a college to be with a boyfriend or girlfriend is like believing in the tooth fairy. Why? Most college students change both major and love interest at least once. But a teenager in his or her first love naturally is sure this cannot, will not, and is not going to happen to his or her noble passion. One client and his girlfriend who'd been going together for four years and absolutely were getting married right after college went to the same school. Eight weeks into the semester his mother called to say that they both were going with other partners.

*Myth Seven: The College Catalog Will Inform You
Whether or Not This School Is for You.*

Not likely. Read enough of them and they become a blur, because if there's one characteristic they share, it's inter-changeability. Diversity, along with availability, is one of the boasts of American higher education—what with two thousand four-year and one thousand two-year institutions. One might expect, therefore, as a professor observed twenty years ago, that browsing through a collection of catalogs would give a heady hint of variety, of intellectual adventures offered by all this educational imagination, and solid answers on how each of these institutions sees its role and purpose and how it differs from the others in developing personal intellect and character.

What one discovers is that with a few notable exceptions catalogs all say the same thing. Education is a status-conscious, follow-the-leader industry in which obvious tub-thumping is bad form, but in which there is always intense competition for students. The catalog and the view book are the chief sales pitches, with the former camouflaged as an internal document. What the public relations department or a dean may write in the section on philosophy may or may not be read by the faculty members or teaching assistants who confront the students in the classrooms. Indeed, some catalogs and view books are farmed-out jobs, glossily packaged by commercial firms who provide the prose content as well as the slick cover.

Things haven't changed for the better in the forty-odd years since the late Harry Gideonse, president of Brooklyn College, said that if the Federal Trade Commission ever started pros-ecuting colleges for false and misleading advertising, there'd be more college than corporation presidents under cease and desist orders.

Myth Eight: You Should Make Your College Selection
Early in Your Senior Year and Have All
Your Applications in by Christmas or Thereabouts.

More than any other bit of brainwashing to which the
public is subjected about education, this manifestation of the
Chicken Little syndrome has made a scramble out of what
should be an unhurried and painstaking process of investigation, self-examination, and deliberate, informed decision.

The sky does not fall in January, February, or March. In the
academic community, only about 80 colleges, mostly Eastern,
can enforce winter application deadlines. They have uniform
Early Decision and mid-April reply dates. For most of them, this
is a useful and necessary practice, but they take only seventy
thousand or so—about 3 percent of the top students—out of
the 2.5 million freshmen applicants. Most colleges use rolling
admissions—acting on applications as they come in—or their
deadlines don't mean much because they don't have the luxury of having two or more applicants for every bed. Never
once, even during the Vietnam draft, have all the colleges
been full.

Of course, if you're one of the thirteen thousand or so going
to one of the Ivies, Little Ivies, or what used to be the Seven
Sisters, you'd better be prompt about getting in your applications. And if you're one of the fifty-thousand-odd headed for
one of the other early-deadline, very selective colleges, this is
also true.

But since the law that governs admissions is supply and
demand, most of the four-hundred-odd good colleges that can't
be that selective are taking students well into the summer,
depending on the flow of applications. If the admissions staff
hasn't filled its class by spring, they're getting pretty nervous
and will often accept applicants they would have turned down
the previous fall or winter.

Myth Nine: Your College Should Be
Bigger Than Your High School.

Contrary to popular opinion, it should be smaller if you're in a large suburban high school. Girls and boys often think ten thousand to twenty thousand bodies will provide a smorgasbord of attentive, attractive members of the opposite sex and lots of activity, especially if high school has been a painful, ugly-duckling stage or if they've gone to tiny single-sex high schools.

The answer lies not in the number but in the kind of people. Every good college is striving for all the variety it can get: in race, creed, social and economic background, and in interests and person qualities. While Virginia and Michigan make as good an effort at this as the private colleges, most state universities admit largely by formulas based on grades, class rank, and test scores. Also, most of their students are state residents who usually are a notch or two below the out-of-staters in ability, and perhaps in sophistication.

The smaller institution is likely to provide more diversity for the same reason that it is easier to know everyone in a small community than in a great city. As one girl who decided after a year at the University of Maryland to transfer to a college said, "I miss the diversity at Maryland we had at Walt Whitman," her high school.

As for activities, while most of the colleges are in the boondocks, most of the people attending them are city and suburban types. Obviously, if life outside of class didn't offer sufficient attractions, they'd be ghost campuses. The truth is that usually there are more things to do on any good campus than one person could take advantage of.

Myth Ten: Going More Than 200 Miles Away from Home
Means a Costlier Education and Probable Isolation.

It may be cheaper to go six hundred, eight hundred, or a thousand miles away if doing so improves the campus job opportunities or helps get financial aid. Indeed, as discussed in Chapter 6, with some aid packages it can be cheaper to go far away to an expensive college than to live at home and go to a free or low-cost public institution. Furthermore, travel costs may not be nearly as great as parents fear. If the student is in a good school, trips home will be few even the freshman year, because the library should demand some weekend time. After the freshman year, they may be only two a year. And availability of an airport is often more relevant than the distance in miles from home.

Myth Eleven: If You're in the Top 10 Percent of Your Class in a Good, Big High School and Have SATs of 1,300 or Better, You Belong in an Ivy or Little Ivy School to Get the Kind of Education You Should Have.

It is ridiculous to suppose that any group of schools has more than a miniscule share of the quality market. The teaching is better at many small colleges than at Harvard and the students have to work harder. The two most intellectual colleges—Reed and St. John's—aren't Ivy. And a lot of colleges that accept students without such statistics have high-achieving alumni.

Furthermore, grades and scores by themselves do not open the Ivy or other very selective doors. They can afford to look at the whole person, and mere grade grinds, being a dime a dozen for them, are cast aside. For example, in 1987 Duke rejected 37 percent of the valedictorians who applied, 45 percent of those with verbal scores of 750 to 800, and 55 percent of those with 750 math scores.

Myth Twelve: Ivy League Schools Are Looking for Students Who Don't Have Excellent Grades.

This hardy perennial is a misreading of something that every intelligent admissions officer has always tried to do: attract people who have done something. It is often grasped at by parents of underachievers who may have heard of a much-publicized foundation grant to Williams College in the fifties to finance an admissions-risk program for boys who had achieved outside of school. To be accurate, the myth should read: Good colleges are looking for students who have something to offer *besides* good grades and scores. If that something is impressive enough the grades may not have to be excellent, but they can't be bad.

One of my young friends with an SAT total of just over 1,000 and a C+ average was accepted by Amherst, but after high school he had won a Bronze Star medal in Vietnam and was doing a good job managing a bar. Another with a strong B average excited every admissions director I talked to because he had taught himself calculus in two summers and then took a semester of it and got a B to prove he knew it. He taught himself to play the piano and played Rachmaninoff; sold more tickets to the Boy Scout fair than anyone in the county; was an authority on Appalachian butterflies, and discovered a species new to Maryland and wrote a monograph on it.

Years ago, before Princeton was quite so tough to get into, the undergraduate dean came to me one spring day with what he rightly thought was a good Sunday story for *The New York Times*. He and his fellow administrators had been disturbed to discover, in going over the dossiers of the senior class, that many of the men who seemed most likely to reflect credit on Princeton were persons of accomplishment who otherwise had been marginal admittees, some with SAT scores in the low four hundreds.

Myth Thirteen: SAT Scores Are the Most Important Thing;
Good Ones Will Get You in the Good College
and Poor Ones Will Keep You Out.

Wrong. Most important are good grades in a tough program, and rank in class, especially in a big suburban high school. Rank is not so important in a class of fifty as in one of five hundred. Then come the SAT scores. What an applicant says about himself or herself in the personal statements and essays can be and often is more important than the SATs. A look at the freshman profile of any very selective college will reveal that a quarter to a third of the very highest scorers don't get accepted.

Chapters 11 and 12 will tell you what makes a good high school program and how to judge yourself as an applicant.

A red flag goes up whenever an admissions officer sees high scores and mediocre or poor grades. As a former dean at Oberlin said, "It was always a great temptation to take the kids with sixteen hundred on the College Boards and B averages. But they always were disappointments." In other words they were not workers and proved to be either mediocre or poor students in college. But when grades are higher than the scores would indicate, it means an achiever, and she—more often than a he—has plenty of good choices.

SAT scores are important to the big institutions that admit by formulas based on grades, scores, and class rank. The better the admissions director the less the importance he attaches to SAT scores.

Myth Fourteen: A Coaching Course Will Improve
Your SAT Scores and Hence Your Chances.

No prep course is going to lift a 400-bracket scorer into the 600 level. No matter what else the disputants say in this hotly argued issue, this just won't happen—ruling out some freak occurrence—because the verbal part is a test of the range of a person's vocabulary, how well he can analyze a paragraph, and his ability to handle analogies. Naturally, no quick fix can do the work of a long habit of reading good books. A seventeen-year-old who has had little interest and little practice in these skills for eleven school years isn't likely to become adept in a few weeks.

The verbal score and the amount and kind of reading a

person has done are like ski tracks. I've never known a non-reader to have a high verbal score, nor a good reader to have a low one.

What is "good" reading? It's not just anything between book covers. Too many teenagers share that mistaken belief with a young friend who had a verbal score of 45 on the PSAT but who insisted that he "read a lot." "What kind of things?" I asked. "Fantasy, action, *Red Star Rising*, things like that." I handed him a compilation of the kinds of books read by kids who'd gone to Mount Holyoke over the last few decades. He studied it for a minute or two and with a look of incredulity asked, "These are books kids actually read in their spare time?"

If a prep course is long enough and requires enough homework it usually helps the very low scorers—if they really work at it—to improve their vocabularies and reading and test-taking skills. Since the test is of "developed ability," as the Educational Testing Service (ETS) says, the longer and more demanding the course, the more it's likely to help. Youths with a reading habit aren't as likely to be helped much since they already have the tools and tend to score in the six hundreds or better anyway. And I've known of some clients whose scores have dropped after a prep course. A prep course is much more likely to boost the math score, and ETS has long said it is helpful to be taking a good math course at the time.

If, after a prep course, one's scores go up thirty or forty points each in the verbal and math, nothing has really been accomplished, for normal growth will account for that much annual improvement. And that small a rise is not statistically significant; that's why colleges report application scores in brackets of fifty. Rarely have I known of one-hundred-point increases in the verbal score, and they were unusual cases. In one, a boy worked hard for ten weeks and raised his score into the four hundreds. Another, who had had a learning difficulty, was drilled for several weeks on the Latin roots of words and brought his verbal into the five hundreds.

As for freak scores, Tom Anthony, Colgate's admissions

dean, said he had a case where an applicant had scores of 1,000 and 1,100, and senior scores over 1,400. The last scores were tossed out as obvious misfits. "There was also nothing in the application," he said, "to validate such high scores. This would not be an unusual reaction."

Myth Fifteen: A Bad Recommendation
from a Teacher or Counselor Will Ruin Your Chances
of Getting into a Good College.

It cannot if what the teacher or counselor says is not true, and sometimes even if it is true. So parents, don't be afraid: criticize the bad teacher; take a stand against the injustice or the stupidity. Too often a bad school problem goes uncorrected because parents fear that complaining will imperil their child.

One negative opinion running counter to the general estimate of a student won't hurt him any more than one bad grade, probably less. The admissions director is going to look at the whole picture. If there is a teacher conflict and a bad grade, or the prospect of a bad recommendation, deal with it honestly, putting all the cards on the table in the application. That will do two things: impress the admissions director because there's nothing so refreshing and winning as candor, and help take the steam, if any, out of the negative comment, particularly if it is unwarranted.

Remember, admissions directors are sensible people aware of failings in teachers as well as in students, and they don't believe everything they read. As one of the Little Ivy admissions directors said, "I always apply the filter factor."

Myth Sixteen: Your Choice of Major Will Decide
Your Career Path. Therefore, the Quality of
That Department Should Govern Your Choice of College.

This mistake has led many people into the wrong choices. One of the most overrated things about college is the imagined importance of the major. There's only one chance in ten that a person will be doing anything connected with his college major ten or fifteen years out of college. That's what every survey of alumni finds. Furthermore, since most eighteen-year-olds know very little about themselves or the world, and nothing about what variety of choices may be open to them a decade ahead, the versatile preparation of a liberal education is the most practical course and early specialization the least.

Indeed, an early choice of major ought to be resisted or avoided so as to spend a couple of years sampling around and getting a broad groundwork. Most students change direction at least once, often twice. Besides, no matter what the major, four years of college won't produce a practitioner in any field that isn't mere formula and routine. Medical schools care only about the biology, chemistry, physics, and math required for admissions, and often would prefer a nonscience major. There's no such thing as a prelaw major; no first-rate college even has an undergraduate journalism major; and if you want to be an anthropologist or archaeologist, the graduate school would prefer a history major.

In engineering, the area that demands the earliest full commitment, the attrition rate is highest. Nationally, about 30 percent finish the course.

The choice of college should be governed by what the ethos and the intellectual force of that place seem likely to do for you as a person.

Myth Seventeen: A High School Diploma Is Needed to Get into College.

Heavens no. I've had a few clients go on to college at the end of their sophomore years, and a lot at the end of their junior years. The sophomores have been very bright and voracious learners. Juniors have no problem if their records are good, they're socially mature enough, and another year in high school would be a bore or a waste. Good colleges have been doing this for a long time, but they do it on an individual, case-by-case basis.

For the nineteen-year-old and older, the General Educational Development (GED) Test will do quite nicely, even if one has never set foot in a high school. Years ago, a twenty-two-year-old who had dropped out in the ninth grade not only got into and did well in college, but also reached the final cut for a major graduate award. And the GED alumni do well in college; they're motivated.

Myth Eighteen: Going to a Private Prep School Will Enhance Your Chances of Getting into a Good College.

Quite often the opposite is true. While a few of the most prestigious prep schools may have Ivy graduates as college counselors as well as doing a nonpareil job in the classroom to give their kids an edge, a high rank in a big, competitive suburban high school is usually a lot more persuasive to any admissions officer than high rank in a small private school. A Little Ivy admissions director once said,"Walt Whitman [in Bethesda, Maryland] is the best high school in the United States; at least I get more good students from there."

The highly competitive private school can be a liability if a good student winds up with a much lower class rank than he would have had in his public school. The private schools are of such variable quality that the college admissions director wants to know whether it's tough or easy. If a transfer from a public school is getting markedly better grades at the private one, it will look like a trade of high tuition for high grades.

Myth Nineteen: Millions of Dollars in Unused Scholarships Are Going Begging Every Year.

This pie-in-the-sky story has been popping up every year for thirty years. It benefits the sellers of books on how to find scholarships and, with the cost of private colleges soaring, has

spawned a cottage industry of so-called financial aid consul-
tants who promise to "find" sources of aid, help fill out the
college's financial aid form as adroitly as possible, or help
shuffle assets around to appear eligible for aid.

The truth is that there never has been more than a fraction
of the money needed and applied for every year. At least 95
percent of all aid is channeled through the colleges. Unless
one has veteran's benefits or works for a firm with a scholarship
program, the chance of finding much money outside the college
channels is pretty slim to none. The various garden club, Legion
posts, and so on that do give "scholarships" do so in pittances
that would barely pay for a semester's textbooks. As Chapter
17 will tell you, the financial aid office of the college that accepts
you is the best place to go for help. That's what those folks
want to do, free.

Myth Twenty: A Good College Is Hard to Get Into.

Even at the crest of the college-going boom and in the haven-
seeking panic of the Vietnam War this was a myth. Anyone—
whether he or she is a poor student, a problem learner, an
average or a good student—can have choices of places that
will help him or her grow. That's what this book is all about.

2
College,
A Buyer's Market

More Than One Good One
Is Looking for You.

I once asked an acquaintance who had been raised in Wisconsin why she had gone to Radcliffe. "In the middle of my high school career," she said, "I met a boy from Princeton who told me I should go to a certain good women's college in the East. But when the time came to decide, all I could remember was that its name began with an R, so I got a list of colleges, saw the name Radcliffe, and that was it."

In those quiet days before 1950, she, like her friends, could apply to only one college. As was the custom, a high school senior or her parents decided on a school, sent in the application, and that was it. It was a buyer's market; it took no show of brains or grades to get into an Ivy League school. Nor was there all this agonizing over personal statements and essays. But shortly thereafter it was a different world and a different struggle. Had she been a few years younger, she would have been part of the post-World-War-II baby boom and caught in the college-going frenzy of the fifties and sixties. And unless

21

she had been a whiz kid, she wouldn't have dared to be so cavalier as to apply only to Radcliffe.

But since the early seventies she could have gotten into the school of her choice or one just as good. And that is perhaps the best-kept secret in higher education. There is a buyer's market in high quality colleges. True, a tiny number are as hard and sometimes harder to get into now than during the sixties. But for every one of these there is another college just as good and sometimes better for a given individual which is looking for students. However unfashionable it may sound, it is the quality of the undergraduate experience, not the name of it, that powers the productive life.

The central message of this book is that there is a lot of non-Ivy quality available and for many different kinds of students, not just for those aspiring to the Ivies. Chapter 10 will list some of my favorites and many additional ones that can make a difference.

By 1973, the admissions picture had so changed that a student with a C+ average and a total of 850 on the Scholastic Aptitude Tests (SATs) could get into 85 percent of the two thousand four-year colleges. The run of the mill and a lot of public institutions were accepting applicants who did not even have C averages in high school. Up the scale, colleges that in the boom days could demand a half-A, half-B average and high class rank had to be content with half-B, half-C averages and much lower class rank.

In 1987 and 1988, an upward blip in the numbers going to college, which fooled the demographers and baffled the admissions people, made many of the better colleges somewhat more selective. In 1989 there was some leveling off, however, and the census forecasts are for a shrinking teenage population until 1992—and a more and more favorable buyer's market.

Because there is not always a correlation between selectivity and quality, it is worth repeating that anyone rejected at a Radcliffe or an Amherst can get into another school that can do as much, maybe more, in helping one realize his potential. For example, two of the most intellectually demanding colleges in the land—Reed and St. John's—aren't competitive most years. They are self-selective; unless the applicant has a commitment to learning for the sake of learning and not for the sake of grades, he'll find he's made a mistake. Since so few are willing to pay that kind of price, Reed has often taken 95 percent of its applicants and St. John's 85 percent or more, whereas Radcliffe or Amherst skim off 18 to 20 percent. Similarly, several of the colleges that produce the highest percentages of future Ph.D.'s and *Who's Who* alumni accept anywhere from 70 to 90 percent of all who apply. You will find some interesting research results on this in Chapter 8.

Faculty members at Reed who have taught at Ivy League institutions, when asked if they noticed any difference in the two groups of students, invariably say something like, "All the difference in the world. There they were learning for the sake of grades; here they're learning for the sake of learning." The inference is easy: the community where learning is valued for its own sake is much more likely to affect the development of values and the ability and desire to go on learning and to grow than is the community where learning is a means, not an end.

The message that there are many little-known keys to the good life is similar to Keats's observation that "Full many a gem of purest ray serene, / The dark unfathomed caves of ocean bear." But it is a message that is faintly heard for many reasons. Among them are the recent college-going boom, the failings of counseling, the lact of consumer research on colleges, indolent consumerism, and the "designer-label college" syndrome.

Education was destined to become a twentieth-century growth industry. The country's enormous economic and population growth, its vast wealth and commitment to education for all, and the vast growth of knowledge in every field all helped to ensure that. Only about 10 percent of the teenage population went to college just before World War II. Then the GI Bill opened the door to the hundreds of thousands of returning veterans. By the end of the Korean War the boom was on, nearly swamping the colleges. The percentage hit fifty, and higher education became a seller's market, such as that the automobile dealers had after World War II when Detroit's assembly lines worked around the clock to satisfy the national hunger for cars instead of tanks.

From then on, college became a consuming family anxiety. In 1958, at the height of the tension, an official of the College Entrance Examination Board, who had spoken the night before to a packed house of parents at a New Jersey suburban high school, was asked by a reporter if there was much concern about his subject, the SATs. He replied, "If you could have plugged in that audience, you'd have lit up the whole town." Twenty years later he would have much the same response.

The boom was driven by the certain knowledge that a bachelor's degree was a union card, the requirement for first-class citizenship in the American economic establishment. Just going to college wasn't sufficient; one had to stay the course or else. And those who didn't believe it were soon enough, and usually painfully enough, made converts. There are countless variations on the 1960s story of my friend Bobby. Because he didn't take his comprehensive exams, he didn't get his degree, but he was nevertheless unconcerned. With four years of college on his record, he was confident he would zoom right to the top in his chosen field, the construction industry. After months of toil he was still a laborer with no prospects, so a friend got him a job in a major insurance company, which surely would be more appreciative. Again, the story was the same: no degree, no place on the ladder. So he quit his job and with considerable pain and toil went back and got his degree. All of a sudden he was on the ladder, climbing, and twenty years later was in the company's upper middle management.

Likewise, high school graduates who couldn't wait to make Head Start hum or reinvent the wheel discovered pretty quickly that the world judged them fit only for menial jobs; enthusiasm wasn't enough. One woman, Doris, was so impatient to help the world that she decided not to go to college, but she was back in my office three weeks later, chastened and ready to spend some time qualifying herself to make a contribution.

The war in Vietnam intensified things by making college a haven from the draft. Almost any college looked good. Under all these pressures, the higher education plant was much over-built, but the teenage population never reached the demographers' predictions. Neither did a long-predicted faculty shortage that had caused institutions to stockpile young Ph.D.'s. Thus when the Vietnam War ended there was a surplus of buildings and teachers and a looming shortage of students. Pretty soon it was apparent (to anyone who took the trouble to find out) that a C+ student was a very desirable commodity, and that there were relatively few colleges that wouldn't welcome him. However, students found it hard to make the bold surmise that the market had shifted in their favor, and that they had open to them a variety of good choices. There was plenty of evidence: Ph.D.'s had become such a drug on the market that able young scholars from the best graduate schools couldn't get teaching jobs. Any college not already locked into a bind where most of the faculty had tenure could fill its ranks with able young scholars. And some states discussed closing down unneeded institutions. Colleges huckstered even more aggressively for applicants.

Nevertheless, dropout and transfer rates remained as bad as in the fifties and sixties, with only three to four students in ten in the same colleges after four years. The range of good options open to even the ordinary student was much wider, but obviously many students weren't making the kind of informed choices they could

It isn't surprising that parents, students, and counselors have developed a supplicant rather than a hard-nosed consumer mentality. College catalogs habitually say, "Application should be made early in the fall of the senior year," and high school counselors, who should know that it is a buyer's market, help continue the seller's market mind-set by pressuring students to get their applications in early, when for most colleges this is not only unnecessary but usually penalizes the student.

Why? Because while it is essential that the young buyer examine and test the merchandise (by making working-day, overnight visits to the colleges, as outlined in Chapter 7), it takes time to do this, and most colleges are on rolling admissions; that is, they act on applications as they come in and continue to admit until they're overbooked. In October, November, and December, the applications may be coming in at a rate that augurs two applicants for every bed, which may induce delusions of selectivity and result in rejecting some early applicants. But in February, the flow may be a trickle, and most of those accepted usually choose other colleges. It's a fortunate college that gets a 50 percent yield. Thus the admissions director, faced with the prospect of empty beds and qualms about his job, may find applicants that he would have turned down in November very attractive. As one of the veterans in the business said at lunch one April day even before it became a buyer's market, "I'd be happy to see some of those people I turned down last fall come through my door now."

Admissions directors, incidentally, are the most nomadic group in our society, more so even than football coaches. Both groups live and die by the numbers. Every private college has financial worries, and if the sales office isn't filling the beds, it becomes the scapegoat. (Nearly every new college president thinks a new admissions director is going to bring in hordes of new students. It seldom works that way, however.) Of course a college would love to have its freshman class filled and guaranteed by Thanksgiving or Christmas, but many of them won't fill up until late summer, if at all. There are perhaps as many as four hundred of the two thousand colleges that can be called good ones, and ever since the seventies the majority of them have been taking applications well into the spring and often into the summer. Only seventy-odd of the most selective ones can enforce early winter deadlines. However, large public institutions often have arbitrary cutoff dates because they don't have to depend on tuition income as private colleges do.

The variations in quality, ambience, and ethos can be seen only by asking pointed and embarrassing questions of administrators, students, and faculty members in day-long, overnight visits to at least two or three colleges. This takes time. Some of it should be done in the junior year, but because kids change so much so fast, it is important that they do some more comparison shopping in their senior year.

With counselors pressing for hasty decisions, much too little of this is done. Inevitably, the situation produces anguish. Every winter I get anxious calls from parents whose children have applied to the wrong colleges and fear the game is up because a counselor has warned that it's too late—but counselors should know better.

Once in a while I hear that a counselor has told a youngster that he or she is not college material. That should be forbidden; it's cruel and almost never true. Every high school should have a sign prominently displayed that says, "If you can make it here, you can make it in a college." The truth is that anyone who graduates from any kind of a decent high school in a college prep program, and a lot who don't, can get into many colleges and can have a good college experience. They may have to take summer school courses or go to a junior college first, but one way or another, the door is open to just about everyone who's willing to make the effort. I've seen students with verbal scores in the low three hundreds, bad high school records, and many with learning problems make it through college. In fact, I know of one with a 317 verbal score who graduated from Amherst.

After I'd vented my gripes one day about admissions directors' heavy reliance on SAT scores to the late Eugene S. (Bill) Wilson, Amherst admissions dean, he said,"Several years ago in our freshman football game with Williams we had a tackle who spent the afternoon in the Williams backfield. A Williams admissions officer nudged a faculty member next to him and said, 'See that boy; he won't be back next year. He only had a three-seventeen verbal.' But he was, and in the next three years spent three more afternoons in the Williams backfield and graduated. I knew he could do it because he and another boy in the same high school had identical records in the same heavy schedule and the other boy had a verbal score in the six hundreds."

Also, doors once closed to the underachiever are now open, as they are to the sinner, and fortunately, to the student with a learning problem. In the seventies and early eighties, programs to help students with learning disabilities and problems mushroomed, and often it has been harder to get a place in one of those new programs than to get into the college itself, so popular have they become. It only took the public discovery of the word *dyslexia* to reveal all manner of related problems in need of help. In many colleges, help without formal programs is given by caring faculty members who may not be specialists but who are effective teachers. A student who has dyslexic problems may not only get a good deal of one-on-one tutoring, but he may also be permitted to take his exams orally and to taperecord papers. This concern for the youth with a learning problem is partly a new concern for the customer in a buyer's market.

Large universities have aid available in learning centers or even formal programs. But the instructor in the classroom may not be part of or even sympathetic to the effort, as one of my young friends learned to her sorrow. Convinced she'd have more social life if she went to Tulane, she chose that school over one of the good small colleges we discussed. She had made a 3.2 average in a competitive high school, despite her learning disability, but at the university she got no help from the learning center or the professors and couldn't make her grades. And she had to spend so much time studying that she had no social life. Her father said the learning center's director saw the job as educating the faculty. At a good small college, the girl's teachers would have given her extra time for exams or otherwise helped her along. Their concern is for the undergraduate, their only reason for being. It is not only a matter of mission but also of the profit motive—a job.

And when there is such collaboration, the student is much more likely to be able to conquer his problems. I have had young friends with a wide spectrum of handicaps make it through college and with steadily increasing ability. One, whose dyslexia wasn't discovered until he was in the eleventh grade in a New England prep school, got help and worked at his problem and has long since graduated from Ohio Wesleyan. Another who was certified as legally blind in high school and who did a lot of work with tapes made an impressive enough record at Hiram College to get a graduate fellowship at Carnegie-Mellon. And they are just two of dozens with just about every conceivable kind of learning disability who have done well in college and have been done well by the college.

The underachiever, whose options were often limited to junior colleges in the sixties, now, thanks to the shrinking supply of seventeen- and eighteen-year-olds, can get into colleges that wouldn't have looked at him in the past. And if the underachiever or the sinner has good test scores, his range of choices is broader now.

Late spring or summer applications are often a must for the marginal applicant or someone with a learning problem simply because the college wants as much recent information as it can get. The marginal applicant is usually the underachiever. I have cases every year where an admissions director will say after I've gone over the client's folder, "Let's wait and see how he does when all the returns are in this June, and then call me." And unless the client has stopped working, he usually gets in. This sort of thing happens at colleges of varying degrees of rigor. A C− student may be on his mettle to make Cs and Bs, or a B+ student to improve on a D or a C grade from the previous term. The point is that many colleges are eager to open the door way past Christmas.

The winter deadlines are for the 3 percent who have straight A or nearly straight A records, SAT scores totaling over 1,200, several Advanced Placement or Honors courses, programs that show four years each of math, science, language, and English, as well as substantial out-of-class achievements.

The phrase "substantial out-of-class achievements" is crucial. Parents too often say, "With her grades and test scores she can get in anywhere." Absolutely and positively not so. Many an applicant with straight As and 1,500 on the SATs and nothing else has been rejected by colleges a lot less selective than Harvard or Princeton, for that kind of record indicates a grind, which means an undesirable. The admissions director at Carleton reacted to one such of my clients with, "That kind goes on the heap pretty fast." Carleton takes about 60 percent of its applicants—all of whom are excellent students—compared with 18 to 20 percent by Harvard or Princeton. On the other hand, Carleton often has more National Merit Scholars than any college in the country.

For the vast majority there is a lot more time to shop. And if they take the trouble to investigate some of the colleges with rolling admissions like Eckerd, for example, they may encounter stimuli that will do more for them in the long run than a Cornell or a Penn will do for the other 3 or 4 percent.

The shopping should be done with the right attitude, not "Am I good enough for the college?" but rather "Is it good enough for me?" And in order to decide the student has to confront himself with some basic questions, such as "Why am I going? What do I want of this experience?" This will be discussed in the next chapter. The consumer approach is the only sensible one not simply because college is expensive, but because that experience can develop a person's ability to think critically and imaginatively, to make informed, intelligent connections, and to develop a value system that will affect the kind of person he becomes. It will also give him the prepared brain that can visualize and seize new opportunities. Serendipity.

The undergraduate college's superior potency has been demonstrated by a good deal of comparison of institutional productivity in recent decades, which is described in Chapter 8.

Tabulations of the baccalaureate origins of people who had achieved listings in *Who's Who*, done in the late fifties and again recently, show the entries crowded with graduates of little-known and not very selective colleges.

The good college will also be seen as the fertile seedbed for the nation's thinkers as well as doers. In spite of much evidence to the contrary, Congress as well as most laymen had always assumed that the famous big universities were the source of the nation's scientific and intellectual strength. Consequently, they got most of the Federal funds for science education and research. But recent digging into performance records has revealed that the good small colleges are giving the nation the most brains for the buck.

News stories of Harvard's three hundred and fiftieth anniversary made much of the line, "Its faculty has produced 27 Nobel laureates." Not so. Twenty-four graduated from other colleges, 7 from City College of New York. In the eighty-four Nobel years up to that point, the most sought after college in the land had produced only 9, and all 8 of the Ivies only 27 of the 137 American laureates. The Little Ivies—Amherst, Wesleyan, and Williams—struck out. Little Swarthmore had produced 6; Oberlin, 3; and Wooster, 2.

The popular conception may be that the Washington establishment is peopled chiefly with Ivy Leaguers, but the reality is somewhat different. Nearly 150 Franklin and Marshall graduates, for instance, are influential members of Congress, staff experts, or government officials. One was President Reagan's last chief of staff. Another is Representative William Gray, chairman of the House Budget Committee and, as Majority Whip, second-ranking Democratic leader. As a likely future candidate, he could also be the first black president.

Similarly, Reed, with about eleven hundred students or about half the size of F&M, has about an equal number of alumni in prestigious and intellectually demanding Washington jobs. The immediate reaction to this—that they're old-boy networks—may be true. But their existence also means that faculty members take an interest in individual students, that the students perform on the job, and that they in turn have confidence in their schools' products and therefore can afford to continue populating the network.

The good small colleges are even better door-openers to graduate and professional schools. The graduate department chairman who reads the applications often has gone to one of these small schools. He knows that in the university the undergraduate is a second-class citizen who gets cheated with big classes, much graduate-assistant teaching, and faculty whose interest is in research and publishing and working with Ph.D. candidates because that's where the pay and prestige—and job tenure—are. He knows that the small college faculty member who recommends a student has probably worked closely with him, whereas in a university the professor may barely know the student. And he knows that students from these colleges have done well not only as graduate students, but also in their careers.

Acceptance records to medical and graduate school support this. In some recent years, for example, Antioch and Wooster both have had 100 percent medical school acceptance rates, compared with a 33 percent rate for all colleges. The University of Wisconsin medical school will accept Beloit juniors. Many of the colleges that aren't very selective have medical school acceptance rates over 80 percent, so it boils down to a matter of the applicant's own performance. A good record at any one of scores of good small colleges is better than a lesser one at Harvard.

If these unknown schools are so good, why aren't they deluged with applicants? There are several reasons, any one of which may be enough to turn up a teenager's nose. First off, most people are provincial; to Easterners, a college not in the Northeast—except for California, Colorado, or Florida—is suspect, and so is the region. And almost anywhere, a high school senior may be challenged for wanting an out-of-state college. Anti-South prejudice is less now than it was in the sixties and seventies, but the Midwest still suffers from some vague image of its being a vast prairie inhabited by hayseeds who've never been out of their counties.

Another is the Eastern mystique: if it's in the East, it's not only better but its student body is more sophisticated. To the students living on the East Coast it may be closer to home and the teenager has probably heard of it. Indeed, to the millions along the Atlantic seaboard, anything in the East is closer than anything west of the Appalachians; a father once questioned my credibility for telling him that Cleveland was closer to Washington than Boston. So many clients have objected to exiling a child to the Chicago or St. Louis area but have found New Orleans, Miami, or Portland, Maine, comfortably close that it gives rise to Pope's Law of Geographic Distances: Any distance west from Washington is twice the same distance north or south.

And remember the myth that anyone with a grain of sense knows—a school you've heard of has to be better and safer than one you haven't. There's also the adolescent embarrassment that one's friends have never heard of it. When a college gets its name in the papers, parents start asking about it.

The sheep instinct is responsible for the "hot college" syndrome that lets the bargains go unnoticed. Like teenage dress fashions, its rationale is that the college is acceptable because one's peers approve, or are talking about it. The sheep instinct is a status affliction that short-circuits thinking and alters perceptions. It is often transmitted from this year's college freshmen back to their high schools' seniors and juniors and thence to parents. It makes a school that no one may have heard of five years ago seem very desirable all of a sudden and a key to the good life, however pedestrian that school remains academically. Worse, this affliction obscures the variety of good choices that are available, even to the below-average student, in a buyer's market vastly superior in diversity and quality to pre–World War II days.

Finally, there is the Groucho Marx syndrome of "I wouldn't

belong to any club that would have me as a member." In the
worried sixties, a young client, who I'm sure had never heard
of Groucho's crack, blurted out when I told him Knox College
would accept him, "It can't be any good if it would take me."
While his outburst was unique, his reaction was a fairly common one. After having been brainwashed for two decades by
a seller's market into believing that any reputable college plays
hard to get, many people continue to find the idea of easy
acceptance suspect. And for a teenager with a fragile self-image
because he or she is not in the top part of a competitive high
school class and so can't hope for one of the popular schools,
it is especially difficult to believe.

As the college-age population diminishes, the average student will have more and more good choices if he will only
open his eyes and his mind and look, unafraid of his peers'
opinions. But as one exasperated mother said, "All these kids
want is designer-label colleges."

And that's too bad.

3 🖎

What Are You
Going for, Really?

Confront This Honestly,
or It's Blindman's Bluff.

Peeople are slow learners. The condition, known as cultural lag, means that it takes a long time for them to see a Mozart, a Frank Lloyd Wright, or an I. F. Stone as great rather than as eccentric, or even to appreciate what's going on right under their noses. It took a couple of years, for example, for the American public to get an eye-opening look at the Reagan administration's secret dealings with Iran. Much worse, the crucial business of choosing colleges continues to be a game of blindman's bluff for most teenagers year after year.

One reason is that, as a panel of educators reported in a major study of undergraduate education, many students go with only vague notions of what an undergraduate education is all about or where it is supposed to lead. Those academicians would have been delighted to hear the startling supporting testimony of one of my young clients. A top student, debater, editor, and athlete, he had crossed the country to talk about college and colleges. Yet when we were deep in discussing the pros and cons of various selections, he blurted out, "Well, it's four years out of my life, anyway!" In other words, this was some necessity he had to make the best of. (As a senior at Stanford in 1989 he wrote, "I am a bit aghast that I said those words.")

Another is the fog surrounding the search. The process is confusing; so testified nearly half of the five thousand college students questioned for *College, the Undergraduate Experience in America,* by Ernest L. Boyer, head of the Carnegie Endowment for the Advancement of Teaching, the most comprehensive study yet made of U.S. colleges and universities. They said there was no sound basis for making a decision. One reason is our woeful lack of consumer research on colleges. The other is that few teenagers do any research on themselves. They don't confront the question of why they want to go to college in an intellectually honest way.

Doing that requires some self-examination plus a readiness to recognize what's there. That may take a little work but it's worth it since what happens in college powerfully affects the quality of a person's life, as will be shown in Chapter 9.

Most adolescents obviously expend more effort on learning how to water-ski or how to earn a driver's license than in making an informed choice of college. Otherwise it wouldn't be the case that each year about 2.5 million freshmen enter college but each year only about 975,000 seniors graduate. That's a production rate of a little better than one third. Furthermore, of those who do stay, many persist unhappily to graduation, unaffected and disaffected, unaware of what they've missed. Credentials are all they have to show for a barren marriage.

The first order of business in making a profitable college investment is to heed the injunction "know thyself." And that's what this chapter is about. Hence it is addressed primarily to the student (the next chapter is for the parents' reassurance). Any intelligent parent already knows what I'm going to say and would tell the teenager the same things if only he didn't suffer the communication handicap of being a parent. Nevertheless, the parent should try to get the idea across, but not too hard; overkill is an occupational hazard of parenthood.

It takes both clarity and courage to look at oneself probingly and then to make decisions based on what one sees there and not be influenced by friends or classmates. In more than twenty years of talking to high school juniors and seniors, I have learned that many of them lack any clear idea of what kind of lives they want to lead. Consequently, they are taken by surprise when I ask them what their abilities, strengths, and weaknesses are, what their goals in life are, and what they would say if they had to decide right now how they would like to spend the working hours of their lives for the next ten years if they could not change in that time. And these are children of affluent professional, often prominent, parents.

If the student doesn't look to himself, he's vulnerable to herd thinking, one of the principal causes of bad decisions. For example, when 120 seniors in a class of 500 at Churchill High School in a Maryland suburb of Washington, D.C., apply to Indiana University and ignore such first-rate places in that state as Earlham, Wabash, DePauw, Notre Dame, and Purdue, that shows appalling evidence of a sheep mentality at work in which a lot of adolescents are making blind and probably wrong decisions. Similarly, when 65 in a class of 400 mostly able students at nearby Walter Johnson High make the mass-production state university or one of its provincial satellites their choice, and another 50 apply to like institutions out of state, a lot of good kids are shortchanging themselves—permanently.

This happens all over the country. In one of countless such instances around the country each year, a valedictorian in Memphis's best high school was regarded as a traitor of sorts because she broke ranks and chose Ohio Wesleyan over the University of Tennessee. Nor could friends or teachers in Seattle understand why a promising boy wanted to go away from Washington.

The student must do his own homework. Neither his parents, his peers, his high school teachers, nor his counselors can do it for him. Indeed, the more he lets others into the process, the greater the risk of botching the job. The worst risk is listening to one's peers. They are the most dismally ignorant of all sources of guidance except for a university athletic recruiter.

What do one's high school peers know about colleges? Next to nothing. They know the names of name schools and that's about it. And while most teachers and counselors "know about" fifteen or twenty colleges, they know little or nothing about these colleges' virtues, faults, or the differences among them. That kind of expertise takes on-the-spot research that high school staff have never had either the money or the time for. Furthermore, many teachers and counselors went to teacher-education institutions, and a rigorous liberal arts education may not be in their experience.

Even more to the point, they don't know enough about the customer to know how the various schools' virtues or faults would affect him. He is the one who has to know himself if he is to make a wise decision.

The homework I'm suggesting can't be completed in one session or one day if the student has never seriously looked into himself. But try it today and let it simmer; think about it; try it again next week.

The first thing to do is ask a silly question:

Why Am I Going in the First Place?

Is it because I wouldn't dare not go; I'd be an outcast if I didn't? Is it because I think it will lead to a good job, because I want to be a doctor or a lawyer or a corporate executive, because I want the social life, good skiing, football weekends, a big city, the bragging rights of a prestige college, or an intellectual challenge and a place that will help me grow?

A great deal hangs on how searchingly that question is asked and how candidly it is answered.

What Do I Want Most Out of College? Least?

This also requires some hard thinking. Is skiing a top priority, or having a city nearby? Does an athletic scholarship outweigh the advantages that might be evident long after the athletic career?

What About the Trade-offs?

Would I rather go to Penn because it's Ivy, it's big and in a city, and I think it might be an easier entrée to a job, or go to Haverford or Kenyon because in the small college I'd be involved in my own education and it might therefore be more stimulating and do more for me in the long run?

Should I pick a Villanova because it's in a city or an Earlham because it's more demanding?

Do I need to be a big fish in a big pond or do I need a more familial atmosphere?

Those are questions to which there aren't any reliable answers until you decide on your priorities, not just for the four-year term but for the forty-year long term.

What Do I Want Out of Life, or in Life, Something Tangible or Intangible?

Do I want a comfortable place in the Establishment and a good country club membership, or to do my own thing? Do I want satisfaction or happiness, and what constitutes happiness?

Am I an acquisitor, a creator, a comforter, a venturer, or a problem solver?

Will I need to be involved with people or not?

Who am I? What are my abilities? What do I have to offer?

These priorities are also questions that a seventeen- or an eighteen-year-old may not be able to answer for himself with certainty, but thinking about them is a start and perhaps some of the later chapters will help in deciding what kind of school may be better for the acquisitor and what kind for the venturer, and whether or not a particular school may pave the way.

Your Greatest Danger

Listening to your friends is not quite as bad as taking drugs, but it sure ruins a lot of college choices. Just say no. Be your own man or woman; it's your life. Every year I have at least a couple of clients who apply to Boston U, Syracuse, the University of Richmond, Indiana University, or some other place not nearly good enough for them simply because in their group those schools are all the cry. And every year I get other clients who went to unsuitable schools because they were the fashion and have flunked out or dropped out after a year or two and have to do the job all over again.

As Plato said, the unexamined life is not worth living. A crucial time to start making it worth living is in this period of deciding where to go. If others are the principal influence, it's blindman's bluff, and that's not the smart way.

And if the decision is to take a year off, that is sometimes the best thing. We'll examine the pros and cons of that in the next chapter.

4 ✍

Should Parents
Let Him/Her
Take a Year Off?

It May Be Just What the Doctor Ordered.

Parents don't even like to think about such a prospect; it gives them the willies. It the youth is already doing less than he should, or than they think he should, they fear a year away from school will surely nudge him over the brink and down the slippery slope. And if he is going along all right, they're afraid the interruption will break the spell. The pronoun is masculine because the male of the species is the one most likely to be getting terrible grades or wanting to get off the conveyor belt for a while to look around.

The good news is that a year off will be the salvation of the underachiever and the focusing and firming of the one who wants off for a while, *if* there is a plan, and *if* it is followed. This salvation is not, like the hereafter, a matter of faith. The efficacy of taking a year off is a demonstrated fact of adolescent metamorphosis. As you'll see later, it's been working like magic, so far as college performance is concerned, for forty years. When I was a college administrator I wanted to impose a year off working on every class of high school seniors before they came to college. The idea was a pipe dream, of course, but after a year out working they would be a different group, more mature, and champing at the bit. Consequently, they would tend to get a lot more out of college.

The bad news is that if the parents chicken out and don't insist that the youth follow his plan, if they let him lounge around the house and sponge off them, they not only will make things worse, they'll interfere with his growing up by providing a crutch instead of a push. More bad news is that parents too often are bleeding hearts, unable to stick with the plan.

There is only one caveat: a few people never do grow up. However, making them accept some responsibility will help; otherwise their tendency to lean will be encouraged.

Having a plan is absolutely essential. The youth's days should be occupied with a full-time job or a serious project; no hanging around the house watching television, driving the car, and living off the parents. The time will have to be accounted for when he does apply to college. Every admissions director will demand it; there's no skipping or forgetting the year, although many think or hope this will be the case.

If the year has been idled away doing nothing, the admissions director will be inclined to say, "Go take some courses; prove that you're ready to work." His rationale will rightly be that the person who spends a term or a year doing nothing much is not likely to be motivated to do much in college either.

Who Should Take a Year Off?

The too-simple answer is a person in one of two categories. In one is the person who feels very strongly he wants to do so and persists in it over a period of many months, and who has a definite plan or a sensible reason he can explain. In the other category is someone whose attitude and performance make it clear that he has no desire to and will not do the work.

In the first case, if the high school senior very much wants to take a year off, it is counterproductive for the parents to push for college. Forcing him or her to go anyway breeds apathy or unhappiness, and the usual consequences are poor performance and failure. I have seen it happen time after time; indeed, it seems to me that the unhappy students I've encountered are either the results of uninformed choice or parental interference, where either parents refuse to let them take a year off or insist on an unwanted college choice or sometimes both. When someone really has his heart and soul set on taking a year off, that will be pretty clear.

But remember that adolescents' attitudes are as changeable as the wind; I've known many youngsters to say in the winter—especially if grades are bad—that they don't want to go the following year. But by spring or summer, when friends are all making their college plans, they suddenly have the urge. And they go.

This changeability makes it important to keep the options open until late summer by going through the selection and application process anyway.

In the other category, when the high school grades have been dropping from alarming to catastrophic, and the senior grades are all Fs and Ds, a year off working and supporting himself may make college an investment rather than a bad-odds gamble. But here we leave solid ground because the youth may have more than the usual problems of this most tortured period of life. It could be a divorce, an alcoholic parent, refusal to compete with a sibling or parent, or an alien social world. He may need sympathetic and perceptive counseling, or a change of venue—getting into a supportive college setting where he can have a successful experience. And the word *successful* is crucial.

However, just because a teenager doesn't seem to do a darn thing about selecting colleges or filling out applications doesn't necessarily mean that he's in the not-ready category. Every late winter and spring, parents echo one doctor's angry threat of a few years ago: "This boy isn't going to college next fall; he's just not ready. He hasn't done a darn thing about filling out a single application!" But his son went that fall and did beautifully. Parents forget that the male adolescent's planning span is only about twelve hours.

A fifth year of high school isn't likely to do the nonperformer—or the parents' peace of mind—a bit of good; he'll be bored and just as unproductive. Nor is sending him to the local community college the answer. There he'd be exposed to the same distractions and temptations as high school; also, since it's a commuter school and the end of the educational line for most of its students, the atmosphere is anything but inspiring or conducive to work. Let him get a job and see how the other half lives and how limited his prospects are!

The following story of a college flunkout, his conversion and salvation, should be an object lesson to parents. This intelligent, likable young man has been a sinner longer than most and expresses himself more eloquently, but his story has universality:

In high school he had a 2.7 average but was capable of a 3.5 or better. After four semesters in an ill-chosen college he was on academic warning; the next semester he was suspended for a term. Later in his junior year he was dismissed for a full year. He went home, got a job as a cook, and had no intention of going back to college for he soon got a raise and within six months had been made supervisor of the restaurant. In less than eight months he was in my office with his parents, wanting to get back in college.

As he said, "There is no challenge; I'm not fulfilled; my life is empty. My friends are intelligent, open-minded, curious, with a sense of adventure; but these people I can't even talk to. All they can see in life is getting a BMW or a Jaguar. I wish now I'd gotten out [of college] earlier. But it was a free ride; I had money, a place to live and have fun and go to class occasionally. I was the life of the party. Now I want to do these essential things: go to class, read, read over my notes, learn."

His parents, one a graduate of Duke, the other of Yale with a doctorate in physics from Chicago, both hold executive positions, but neither shook a finger at him. As long as they

were willing to keep on giving, he was happy to keep on taking. It took the mental shock of exposure to the world to wake
him up.

He was able to get a glowing recommendation from his boss.
He convinced me that he had been affected by maturity's magic,
if long overdue, spell, and I was thereby able to convince an
admissions director or two, with the result that he's getting a
chance at a first-rate college, where he will give a good account
of himself. He will in life, too, as do the others who are thus
born again, for they have learned a lesson the hard way.

Here the admissions directors should get a bow for taking
a chance, as several of them over the years have, on a risk
venture who with his less-than-C average was not legal tender
in the academic world. In another chapter I had some harsh
words for the fraternity, but I've never had a repentant flunkout
who didn't get another chance from at least one good school.

What Kind of a Job Is Good?

The quality of the job is not important except in a negative
sense, as the foregoing story exemplifies: the more menial the
job, the better the therapy. A dull, tedious, or difficult job that
is mentally numbing drives home the lesson that if you don't
want to continue to live like the other half does, you'd better
do something about exploiting your abilities. That's not to say
that if you accomplish something noteworthy, like being pro-
moted to a reporter from copy boy, as one young friend did, it
won't help get you into Amherst in spite of an indifferent high
school record.

If Not a Job, What Kind of Project Is Acceptable?

One can pursue a hobby, a business of one's own, travel, take
a study abroad program, take courses, in fact do almost anything, but the operative word is *do*.

What Does the College Want to Know About the Year Off?

If it's been a job, the kind of work record is very important because the boss can testify to your attitude and performance, which will be as good as a teacher's recommendation, as the college flunkout's story shows.

If it's been some other plan, the admissions people will want to know exactly what you did and why and what you accomplished, if anything.

What you can say you learned from your year off is equally important. If a student has looked at himself it will reveal to what extent that secret ingredient, the process called maturing, has affected him. It produces changes for the good, partly because it not only gives a young person time to take stock of his situation, but also, since he can't go to school for a term or a year, enforces a waiting period for resolutions on the new life to firm and set. When I see a client after a year off working or doing something with a purpose, he's a different person; his eye seems clearer and more direct, his handshake is firmer, his voice is more positive, he has a goal, and most important of all, he has motivation, which is 95 percent of the battle.

In short, a year out in the world teaches a hard lesson and teaches it well and for good; namely, that the unprepared brain is sentenced to the have-not jobs. The frustrations and the ego bruises help the maturing process, unfailingly making converts of the doubters and unbelievers.

How Can Parents Be Sure of All This?

There is plenty of evidence that the young subject wises up. The first great revelation came after World War II, when returning GIs by the thousands made uniformly good records in college, irrespective of how bad their high school grades had been. Almost no one flunked out. It was so dramatic a showing that the vice president of Pennsylvania State University campaigned to have Congress require military service right after high school so as to let youths mature before going to college. He argued that the more mature, motivated students would get more out of college, and the school and the taxpayer would benefit as well from the improved efficiency.

As a result of the dramatic experience with the returning veterans, several of the most prestigious colleges made it a practice in the late fifties and early sixties (when there was a plethora of college applicants) to compel students who weren't doing as well as they should to take a year off, without prejudice, to mature. They always came back.

Several studies have been done more recently on those who drop out once they're in college. At Harvard it was found that most of them returned and earned their degrees. This is what happens with most middle- and upper-middle-class students. It is the students from lower income families who tend to stay out because the problem is money.

What If a Student Doesn't Want to Go to College After a Year Off?

In the rare case of a youth who simply does not want to go to college, the parent might just as well take a deep breath, relax, acquiesce, and wait for time to do its work, which may take another year or more. But the parents must insist that he get a job and support himself, or else the battle will be prolonged or lost. If he goes to college against his will, the odds are that he will do poorly or flunk out; and with a poor record, he will have trouble later on getting into a place he might like. If he stays out and works, he will find, sooner or later, that he'd better get the credentials or be doomed to second-class citizenship in the job world.

Does This Happen Often?

Parents who confront the problem of a child who drops out or who refuses to go think it is a shame that only they bear, a dread social disease. It might comfort them to know that it's the biggest club in the country. Sometimes it seems half the families in the country must have one child who has seceded from the Establishment. At dinner one night with former clients whose oldest son had covered himself with academic honors from Princeton on to a doctorate, and whose youngest son had graduated from a prestige college, the conversation was much about the family trauma over the middle child, a girl who had been a hard-core dropout and a runaway. But she had finally graduated from college. The father said, "I learned three things from that experience: There's nothing you can do about it. It's not your fault. And they do come back." A soft sculpture with that message, done by the artist mother, hangs on a wall in my office. As I exclaimed at the time, "I've been trying to tell parents that for fifteen years!"

What If a Person Never Goes?

Of course, many people make notable contributions or achieve great success in many different fields without ever setting foot on a college campus, or getting a degree. The late great Bill Wilson, longtime Amherst admissions dean, was fond of saying that probably 20 percent of the real achievers in this country never set foot on a college campus. But they are usually the people with an idea or a cause that drives them, and perhaps an extra thyroid gland. They fashion their own educations in their own ways or as adult students.

One of the more dramatic examples was Nicholas Christofilos, the Greek creator of America's atom smasher and discoverer of the natural radiation belts encircling the earth—now known as the Van Allen radiation belts—among other spectacular feats. He won the Franklin Institute's Elliot Cresson Medal for his contributions to nuclear physics. He was not only largely self-taught in physics, but also had to invent his own mathematics to present his atom smasher principle. Three years after American scientists at the Brookhaven National Laboratory had pooh-poohed his ideas as unworkable—they couldn't understand his math—they finally came up with the same idea. Christofilos was the star of the American nuclear physics team until his death in 1972.

So, parents shouldn't be too worried; if their child doesn't have the drive of an extra thyroid gland, he'll soon see that getting the credentials is really the primrose path. If he does have the drive, he either won't need the credentials or he'll get 'em in his own way.

5 🔊
What the Good College Experience Should Be

The good college should train you for nothing and prepare you for everything.   The late Bill Wilson, longtime Amherst admissions dean

One of my early campus visits as an education editor was to Amherst to report on a new kind of college being proposed by the four institutions in the area: Smith, Mount Holyoke, the University of Massachusetts, and Amherst. The plan was to involve the student in his own education by way of a research project under a professor's guidance. That was to form the core of his experience. Seven years later Hampshire College was born, a school which does center the student's work on active learning in a project rather than on listening to lectures.

On the same visit, quite different evidence of the good college experience was being unwittingly testified to in conversations with Amherst students, mostly freshmen. Many of them were disturbed; having won admission to one of the country's most selective colleges, they were asking what they were doing there, what they were being prepared for, what was the object of the enterprise. They could see no specific roles for themselves after graduation, especially if they hadn't made a firm choice of major.

They were neither the first nor the last college freshmen to feel that way. But at a big university, such questions would have been less likely. The students there would probably have felt safely on track in their vocationally oriented programs. If the Amherst students had taken their apprehensions to Bill Wilson, the man who had admitted them, he would have assured them Amherst knew what it was doing and that if their college experience didn't disturb them occasionally, something was the matter.

So would many others in and out of the academic world have said, from Aristotle on. They would have made two points: one, that the student should be involved in his own education for it to be effective; and two, that the experience should teach him to think and should work its way into his values.

John Stuart Mill said that a man is a man before he is a physician or a philosopher or a plumber and that if you make him a reasonable and sensible man he'll make himself a reasonsable and sensible physician or philosopher or plumber. Yale had the same idea about the same time. In 1828 it announced that its undergraduates would get no professional courses because nothing was as practical as good theory or as useful as a liberal education. Professional studies, they said, could come later.

Vocational preparation, whether for engineering, medicine, business, or plumbing, is concerned with the job rather than the person. It does not seek to achieve the liberating and enlightening changes in values, attitudes, and thinking that will help one to lead a productive and fulfilling life. That is only done by way of a liberal education. The vocational route prepares for only the most temporary of temporal satisfactions: the first job. Almost everybody changes jobs in the first years after graduation. And who has a crystal ball clear enough to see his last job? The fact is that for this and coming generations, the odds are overwhelming that it hasn't been invented yet.

Dr. John Lombardi, now provost of Johns Hopkins, said in a commencement address as outgoing dean at Indiana University, "College teaches us the skills for success at any job. When we hear the refrain, 'How come I don't have a job on the day I graduate from college?' we are sympathetic but not overly concerned. Practically all of us are doing things we like to do and want to within five years after graduation."

Liberal arts graduates twenty and twenty-five years out of school invariably testify that it was the attitudes and ways of thinking, not the specific courses or information they got in college, that contributed to their success. This has been the experience of such colleges as Oberlin, Haverford, and Amherst when they polled their graduates in mid-career. These unusually successful men and women said in overwhelming numbers that the liberal arts path was what did it for them. If they had it to do over again they would take more courses in the arts, humanities, and sciences.

The liberal arts message, however, is seldom heard by the high school student who hasn't a chance of getting into an Amherst, the kind of place he envisions as guaranteeing a good job and a successful career. His worries are more acute. If—lacking the perceived leverage of a brand-name school—he doesn't know what he wants to major in and what kind of job he should be thinking about, he often thinks he is imperiling his future.

I have tried to reassure many of them that not only are they not failures, but also that neither their own parents nor most of the successful people in this country had any idea at age eighteen of what they would be doing at age fifty. If they thought they did, nine out of ten turned out to be wrong, because those nine wound up in jobs that had nothing whatever to do with their original college majors, and they were glad of it; they were happy in what they were doing because both they and the world had grown and changed.

When I made this point at a meeting with seniors at the best prep school in Washington, one boy asked incredulously, "You mean just major in the liberal arts?" So far as he was concerned, I was trying to put him in a boat without an engine, sail, or rudder.

When the job market got dismally soft in the seventies, parents were more of a problem than the teenagers. More than once a father has said, "Look at this boy; he's a real problem. He's eighteen years old and has no idea what he wants to do." It almost always turned out during the subsequent interview that the father hadn't known either what he wanted to do when he was that age.

John L. Munschauer, Cornell University's longtime career-development service director, said, "Thirty years in college placement have taught me that the future is uncertain. Choosing a major by trying to outguess the job market is like speculating on corn futures."

The University of Virginia, where most of the students think they are safely locked into career tracks—as do those at most universities—published a 1984 survey of its College of Arts and Sciences graduates three to thirteen years out of school to prove that there is, as the booklet is titled, "Life After Liberal Arts." In an effort to educate high school students and their parents, the College of Arts and Sciences, in collaboration with the Office of Career Planning and Placement and alumni organizations, asked two thousand alumni who had graduated between 1971 and 1981 what their jobs and salaries were and whether their liberal arts background had been an asset or a liability. Young professionals of all kinds gave the same emphatic answers as have older alumni of several liberal arts colleges in earlier such polls: a liberal education was responsible for their success; it had proved to be the most practical and useful. Hardly any of the Virginia alumni were in jobs that had any obvious connection with their college majors, or even with their first-time jobs. Eighty-five percent of them were satisfied in their jobs, and 91 percent said they would recommend a liberal arts degree to undergraduates considering the same careers.

Not only were they working in twenty-four different areas that covered the waterfront, but many of them have had five or six jobs since graduation. One, a marketing manager of American Cyanamid Co., has had eight, and a Chase Manhattan Bank vice president six. The median salary was $30,000. Fourteen percent earned $60,000 or more and 21 percent earned $50,000 or more.

Their jobs included legislative aide to Senator Daniel Patrick Moynihan; a special assistant to the President; senior editor, *Money* magazine; executive director, American Bankers Association; president of a computer systems firm; and lighting designer, Atlanta Ballet—and not one of these six had majored in his field.

Whether they were in systems analysis, television sales forecasting, network editorial production, electronics, or medicine, these very successful young people offered teenagers, and especially their parents, the same advice: stop thinking of college as a four-year ticket to a lucrative job in this or that profession; it doesn't work that way in the real world.

Hardly any of these men and women found it easy to get the first job. They had to work at it, and they experienced all the discouragement, uncertainty, and confusion that liberal arts graduates often complain of. Moreover, five out of six of them hadn't been happy in their first jobs, and within three years, three out of four had changed jobs.

But now they say almost with one voice that college should provide an education that teaches one to think and to solve problems, to write and speak effectively, to work with people, and to gain a broad view of the world. These "liberal arts" skills, they say, may not make it any easier to get the first job, but they are what really matter once a person starts moving up through the ranks.

Eighty percent of the Virginia alumni said that what employers valued most were not the grades, the major, or the graduate degrees, but rather personal characteristics, chief of which were enthusiasm, ability to relate to others, and ability to work independently.

The specific skills they have found most important include oral and written communication, interpersonal skills, problem solving, and critical thinking. The owner of a business consulting firm who had been an English major said, "Communication skills are critical. My ability to analyze the Internal Revenue Code is the same skill as analyzing a poem or short story." The vice president of a graphics design firm said, "After ten years I've just realized what I really learned at UVa, unbeknownst to me while it was happening—i.e., how to think and solve problems. This is the single most important factor in my current success."

In the soft job market of the late seventies, employers had said pretty much the same things to three different colleges that had obtained grants to find out from corporate, industrial, and government employers what made a college graduate attractive to them. Invariably, the employers said it was the ability to communicate with the written and the spoken word, which means being able to think; the graduate's attitude toward work; and having the respect of his or her peers. These were far more important than what so many college students consider the holy trinity: major, grade point average, and name of institution.

One third of the Virginia alumni believed their liberal arts training had given them an advantage over their colleagues, while another one third felt their careers would have proceeded no differently had they pursued a technical degree. Similarly, a few years ago, one of my young friends, an Oberlin graduate, said that she and a Wellesley graduate felt they had an advantage over all their technically trained classmates in Carnegie-Mellon's graduate school of drama because "we had read all the plays."

A business analyst with GTE Telenet Communications who was an English major and who later got a Master of Business

Administration degree said, "I was not able to find a career job until after graduating from business school. However, I now find that my English literature degree gives me a definite advantage over those who have strictly business or technical degrees."

The high school senior who has his mind set on a business major should listen to one of the Virginia alums, a bank vice president now but a biology major in college. He said, "A liberal arts background provided me with an overall understanding of people, politics, and society, which are most important to the understanding of marketing." This is his third job. His first one was as a $7,200-a-year junior high school teacher.

A big reason for their success, which shines through their answers and the advice they give, is initiative. They tell students to get involved in campus activities, but for substance, not for show; to take some career-related courses, to get internships and to have summer work experiences, and finally, to use initiative in investigating career possibilities and in looking for an actual job. Eighty-six percent of them said their own personal initiative was crucial to their being hired for their first job.

The Virginia results, like all similar polls in the past, destroy any basis for one of the most persistent and harmful myths about college; namely, that when you choose a major, you're choosing your career. The reality is that there is virtually no connection between liberal arts majors and future career paths. But in spite of continuing, unarguable proof to the contrary, students and their parents persist in wearing the job-track blinders.

Perhaps the person who takes the liberal arts route is more venturesome, more intellectually curious, and has more get-up-and-go than the one who is seeking safety in the job track. The liberal arts graduate has to sell himself more than the one with the professional degree, and this makes him more alert, juices up his adrenaline, and activates the imagination and gray cells. It stimulates his survival instincts, teaches him to land on his feet, and makes him a better performer and competitor.

MIT's engineering dean evinced such thoughts when, in announcing that the technical school's undergraduates were going to get a lot more exposure to the elements of liberal education, she said, "Too many MIT graduates wind up working for too many Harvard, Yale, and Princeton graduates."

I have boasted for years that I could be dropped blindfolded onto any engineering campus in the United States, with the possible exceptions of Caltech and Harvey Mudd, and in less than half an hour know it was an engineering school. Few students or faculty will be interested in what's going on in the world or on campus. Once, at Carnegie-Mellon, walking down a hall of the newest and most distinctive building on campus, I asked in five successive faculty offices who the architect was. When the fifth one didn't know and I observed that it was the only new and different building around, his reply was, "We tend not to think in those terms." I said, "Don't you think you ought to?"

Faculty members so barren of aesthetic or intellectual curiosity are not likely to contribute much of value outside the tricks and techniques of their trades. This single-track mindset is one reason that in engineering's lean years engineers have so much trouble finding jobs. They have trouble adapting because their preparation has fitted them with blinders.

A dramatic example of how the liberal arts' broad exposures can enable a person to find his true love—or, more precisely, to see that one's current love may really be collateral preparation for the real thing—is the story of one of the ablest and most intellectual persons of any age I have ever known. He was also the only client or friend from whom I ever received a letter with a paragraph of Aristotle's *Ethics* in Greek pasted on the back of the envelope with his translation below it.

An omnivorous reader, he had always considered himself betrothed to the classics and saw himself as headed for a career as a classics professor, which was his ideal of the rewarding life: being a source of intellectual stimulation and passing on the heritage of civilization. Furthermore, a professor at Chicago had told him in his freshman year that he was good enough to get the one classics vacancy that might exist in academia when he got his Ph.D. But like other intelligent youths, he had catholic interests: Dorothy Sayers's detective novels, theories of education, tennis, swimming, and art, and he was a frequent visitor to Washington's galleries.

He didn't like Chicago and transferred to Oberlin as a sophomore and two disturbing things happened—as they are likely to in a good college. He was only two semesters away from a major in Greek when he discovered William Blake, the English artist and poet, and did a paper on him. Second, he fell under the spell of a wonderful teacher who awakened a sleeping passion. For, late in his junior year, he wrote me:

Today I had the extreme pleasure of visiting Ellen Johnson [Oberlin art history professor emeritus] in her beautiful Frank Lloyd Wright home. She is a charming and inspirational woman who overflows with life and love, and her house is so wonderful. It was one of the most inspiring one-and-a-half hours I've ever spent. I only wish I could have taken a class from her. At the beginning she said something that I've always believed, that scholarship and teaching are acts of love and went on to prove this, for when she gave a tour of her home and art collection and pointed to a [painting by] Rauschenberg or Dine or Jasper Johns, et al, all the people who had been troubling me lately, and said, "Isn't it lovely," I had no doubts.

The fact that he is now working on his doctorate in art history, after having had his pick of all the richest and most prestigious fellowships, testifies not only to his abilities but also to the fact that he had the good experience that affects a person's life by helping him find the route he wants to take. He will still be pursuing his goal of passing on the heritage of civilization, but it will be by way of art rather than by way of Greek and Roman literature. And he will be a more broad-gauge, perceptive art historian for having the classics background.

His experience stands out like a city of gold compared with that of another client, a girl from a New York City suburb who made a wrong choice, then transferred after a year. She wrote,

I had no focused idea of exactly what "being educated" entailed. My father had graduated from Hamilton College, and my older sister was completing her junior year there. . . . I chose not to attend Hamilton and accepted a place at Indiana University solely on the basis of its size (24,000 undergraduates) and its location. . . . Going to a large school in the Midwest would be an interesting and exciting experience . . . I wanted to strike out into new territory.

Having spent almost one full academic year at Indiana University has helped me learn more about myself . . . and what kind of education I want. . . . The size of Indiana University, although one of the primary reasons I chose the school, has often been the cause of great frustration to me. Three out of my four classes have well over 100 students in them, which gives rise to little or no interaction between the professor and the students. I dislike the lack of give and take in the classroom. At Hamilton, a class of 20 instead of 200 gives everyone a chance to raise questions and state opinions. . . . Simply taking notes in a lecture hall and spitting them back on an exam leaves little room for growth as a student. . . . At Hamilton I can have a greater chance to get to know my professor, and he or she will know me as more than simply a Social Security number.

Students at a school as large as Indiana often do not feel part of the community. My dorm alone has over 2,000 people living in it, and I sometimes feel that I am living in an apartment building in a large city rather than on a college campus. Although I know a lot of people to say "Hi" to on my way to and from my classes, for the most part my friendship with them is on a very superficial basis.

I would like to become involved in as many different activities in college as I was in high school. At Indiana it is almost impossible to become involved in acting unless one is a theater major, or to work on the *Indiana Daily Student* unless one is a journalism major, or to join the women's track team unless one had record-breaking times in high school. I miss my extracurricular activities. . . .

It is with great regret that I have found that I am not interested in the same subjects the most of my classmates are. . . . I am in the school of liberal arts and they are in the school of business. The Business School at Indiana attracts renowned professors as well as highly motivated students. English and the humanities are, on the whole, considered of a lesser calibre than business courses. The students taking English courses tend to be either fulfilling a requirement or hoping for an easy A (and are often disappointed). I have found few friends who truly love the liberal arts, and while they must be there, I have not found them. I would look forward to being at a school like Hamilton where the humanities and English are truly valued, and where I could be in class with others who feel about them as I do.

She did transfer to Hamilton, where she found more of the shared values she wanted, and which are an essential ingredient of the good experience. An engineer is not going to be happy in the Great Books program at St. John's College in Annapolis unless he's interested in ideas as well as how things work. An artistic Bennington or a venturesome Hampshire student is going to feel strangely out of place in a technical Lehigh or Rennselaer, and vice versa.

A sense of shared values is one mark of a good college, just as it is of a good high school. The inspiring success of an inner-city high school in Richmond, Virginia, in providing an escape hatch from the ghetto for poor kids has been, like others in other cities, a story of shared values. Students and parents made a compact that stipulated four years each of a foreign language, math, and science, in addition to English, history, government, computer science, passing the Red Cross swimming test, and doing community service. The parents agreed to provide study space and quiet for the required two hours of daily study. Every single member of the graduating class went on to college. And they went to Princeton, Duke, Oberlin, Rice, Howard, and Virginia Military Institute, among others. Had it not been for Richmond Community High School, a few of them might have gone to the local community college. The colleges most likely to affect a person's growth operate on the same principle.

If more parents and teenagers had been reading some of the serious studies of the good small colleges, such as *Changing Values in College*, by Philip Jacob, or *The Distinctive College*, by Burton R. Clark, many college choices would have been more wisely made. These two books, among others, show that the colleges that turn out people who accomplish things and who make contributions are places that hold in common values of ethical integrity and of service. They are places with a sense of mission.

They could also have profited from reading Nicholas von Hoffman's *The Megaversity*, for a depressing portrayal of the routine rite of passage that is the lot of the great majority in the universities who aren't good enough students or fortunate enough to be in some special program. It is a routine in which the student has little interest or involvement beyond getting the degree.

The good colleges have a commitment to learning, meaning work; high expectations for both students and faculty; a strong sense of purpose; and a sense of community. Haverford College, which has as productive and successful of body of alumni as any, has been conducting exit interviews of its graduating seniors since 1975 to get their reactions to their four years there. One of the threads that runs through them is their feeling of a strong sense of community. Another, attributable to its honor code, which is both social and academic, is that "trust is the rule." The college seniors say also that Haverford gave them values.

They also have something to say to high school seniors who think they must go to a college larger than their high school in order to have an adequate social and learning experience, a fixation that seems to afflict at least half the young people I talk to. After four years in a school of one thousand students, the Haverford seniors don't think it's too small. College has been for them a time of internal exploration, and the small community is more conducive to that than the large one.

Since Harverford students are not only very intelligent but tend to be more self-sufficient than most, they may more readily appreciate why virtually every good college in the country is smaller than most suburban high schools. Virtually every good college is around two thousand or under for a reason: involvement, something that is hard to come by in the big university. In the college visits of the Carnegie Endowment team for the book, *College*, only 20 percent of the liberal arts college students did not feel a sense of community, whereas at all institutions 40 percent did not.

Involvement is crucial. Alexander Astin, of the University of California at Los Angeles, who has been studying the effects of college on students for thirty years, says small colleges have a greater positive impact on students than large ones, and private ones more than public ones. The small ones rate higher in student achievement than the big ones, and the key is student involvement, both in campus life and in learning.

In gathering evidence for his book *College*, Dr. Boyer's team came to much the same conclusions after talking to five thousand students at all kinds of institutions. They said, "We conclude that the effectiveness of the undergraduate experience . . . is directly linked to the time students spend on campus and to the quality of their involvement in activities." Being in honors programs and undergraduate research programs are also central to productive experiences.

The outstanding records in producing scientists made by fifty small colleges described in Chapter 8 offer some proof. The small colleges dramatically outperformed twenty leading universities, and the key was student involvement in their own education, in this case by way of collaborative student-faculty research.

Dr. Boyer's team documented with some damning statistics the differences between what is likely to be a good and personal experience in a small college and the relatively uncaring and impersonal process of the university They found that few university faculty members carry even half a normal college teaching load. Indeed, at the research universities, 61 percent teach only one to four hours a week or none at all, and at the doctorate granting institutions, 38 percent had little or no contact with undergraduates. Moreover, as he quoted Harvard sociologist David Riesman, "their commitment to research can have a chilling effect on the classroom and be shockingly detrimental to students." The undergraduate is an unwanted, often rejected, or merely tolerated child.

At the liberal arts colleges, 85 percent of the faculty polled by Dr. Boyer's team were interested primarily in teaching, as opposed to 39 percent in the research universities and 60 percent in the public universities. As might be expected, half again as many liberal arts as university students said their professors were interested in their academic progress or encouraged them to discuss their feelings about important issues. Better than nine out of ten liberal arts college students said their professors encouraged discussion in class.

It would have been man-bites-dog news if Dr. Boyer's team had found anything different. Colleges make bragging points of having small classes and professors who love to teach. And good teachers like discussion; it demands mental activity by the student. In fact, one university professor told Dr. Boyer's people that if his own undergraduate math classes had been as large as the one he was teaching, he would never have become a mathematician. In short, the undergraduate is far more likely to get only half a loaf in the university, and the classroom half he does get has a short shelf life.

Involvement means the college provides opportunities for department seminars, tutorials, student research programs, opportunities for interdisciplinary and independent study, jointly taught courses, close collaboration between teachers and the library, and senior theses. These are some of the things that mark the good college experience and that should be asked about when a student visits the school.

Today, off-campus programs, which weren't widely available forty years ago, provide many exciting ways of making the student an active participant. They cover almost every conceivable interest and are scattered around the globe. The twenty-five members of the Associated Colleges of the Midwest (ACM) and the Great Lakes Colleges Association (GLCA), for example, offer study semesters in Africa, India, Japan, Hong Kong, Latin America, Scotland, and Yugoslavia. There are arts programs in New York, Florence, London, and elsewhere. There are internships of all kinds that provide professional experience and that often lead to jobs after graduation.

Students with interests in the sciences or social sciences can be part of research teams at the Oak Ridge and the Argonne National Laboratories. At ACM's Wilderness Field Station at the headwaters of the Mississippi in northern Minnesota students can paddle and portage for two weeks studying animal and plant habitats. Others can intern in local governments, doing urban studies in Chicago or Philadelphia, or in Holland or Yugoslavia if they prefer.

Consortia such as these offer students a variety of off-campus experiences cooperatively that one college couldn't afford to do alone. In the New York arts program, for example, fifty students from the twelve GLCA schools work as apprentices or interns with playwrights and sculptors, as subcurators in museums, as assistant stage managers in off-Broadway productions, or as interns in architectural firms, among others, getting hands-on experience.

They gather regularly at their Upper West Side headquarters where a mostly ad-hoc faculty works with them and where they compare notes and evaluate their experiences. When they return to their campuses their school work has a new meaning, and a valuable experience has been added whether or not they ever become artists or architects or curators. About half the students in the twenty-five colleges have spent a study term or a year abroad or elsewhere off campus by the time they graduate, many times the figure nationwide. Dr. Richard Lambert, director of the National Foreign Language Center at Johns Hopkins, estimates that only one in one hundred nationwide have study terms abroad, and Jane Kendall, director of the National Society for Internships and Experiential Education, says there are no valid estimates on the number of domestic programs, but counting cooperative education programs, perhaps one in four have some kind of off-campus experience.

These are only two examples of the many consortium arrangements across the country that broaden the offerings of individual colleges. Some are more workable than others. The Five College Consortium of Amherst, Hampshire, Mount Holyoke, Smith, and the University of Massachusetts is a prime example of one that does work. Students can take classes at any other institution, and some courses are joint enterprises. Synchronized calendars and class scheduling and a free minibus system that runs at frequent intervals makes it practicable, and over six thousand students a year take courses on other campuses. They really do have at their disposal the resources of four other institutions.

But consortium arrangements aside, virtually every good college has some off-campus and overseas programs, or will help the student make arrangements for them and provide leaves of absence for internships or a term on another campus. There is a general acceptance of these things that did not exist a few decades ago. For many students, taking a term away from school for an internship in a government agency or a business has been one of the most valuable parts of their college experience. And some mention such an experience first when talking about their college days.

Antioch College has offered an experiential education program since 1921. There, students spend alternate quarters in campus study periods and on jobs. Or, they may have creative study projects off campus or participate in a GLCA overseas program. Antioch believes, and so do its alumni (who as a group are among the most successful and productive of all), that if the purpose of college is to help people become independent beings the off-campus jobs and projects do that.

Antioch students, like Haverford's, tend to know who they are and to be self-sufficient human beings, but tend to go Haverford's one better. In fact, I've never encountered a student body as independent and uppity, or as involved, anywhere. The students have a voice in the governance of the college and they exercise it. A meeting on cafeteria prices, which might have drawn a half-dozen students at many colleges, attracted two rooms jammed full there. And the student chairman told the food services managers, "Now Jack, we're not asking for answers; we're demanding them."

In short, what has been working for Antioch students for three quarters of a century is now enriching the experiences of countless others, if on a much more modest scale.

A central ingredient of involvement on the college's side is rigor. If it's easy, it's a sham. And as shown in Chapter 7, it's a fun task to find out how rigorous a place is and what its standards are just by asking a couple dozen students and two or three of the faculty. The students will be eager to talk and most faculty members are stoop-shouldered with honesty and will level with the questioner, even though they work there.

One might assume the more famous or prestigious the school, the more rigorous it is. Not necessarily. How demanding a school is and how much active learning is going on are matters that have a whole lot less to do with prestige than most college shoppers think. A few years ago, a young friend who had been at Princeton a year and a half and then transferred wrote me, "I am finding Macalester very satisfactory. The level of teaching is as high as it was at Princeton, at least in my experience, and one must work about as hard to keep up." And a girl who transferred from Beloit in Wisconsin to prestigious Wesleyan in Connecticut said the difference to her was a cold feeling of every person for himself at the Little Ivy.

But rigor is central to the quality of a school, large or small. A girl who transferred from East Carolina University—a school that was made a university by legislative fiat—to the University of Wisconsin, wrote, "All of my classes are so much more stimulating. It isn't even fair to compare them with the ones at my other school. My grades are good; not all As like at East Carolina, but I'm sure I'll be more proud of whatever grades I earn because I've worked very hard."

Unfortunately, there are a lot more East Carolinas around than there are those of Wisconsin's high standards. Nearly every state has at least one public institution like it or worse, not to mention private ones of easy standards.

Two of the criteria I use in recommending colleges are a predominantly residential student body, and one where a sizable proportion of the students come from outside the college's immediate region. The second one is less important than the first. Knox College, which is a Grade A school by any measure, only has about 30 percent out-of-state students, but it has a cosmopolitan student body, heavily from the Chicago metropolitan area and more Illinois Scholars than any college in the state.

Kalamazoo in Michigan is another gem which if it were on the East Coast would be as selective as almost any other college and a lot better than most of its neighbors, whatever state it was in. Like Knox, most of its students are from its area, but few colleges have as distinguished a record of producing graduates who go on to get doctorates or who achieve mention in Who's Who. Some teenagers are put off by the name, but Kalamazoo is a most attractive city.

The residential character of a college, however, is far more important than the geographical distribution of its student body; it is vital. Without it there can hardly be much sense of community; the experience will be more like an extension of high school. It is much more difficult either to establish or maintain any real student-faculty friendships at a commuter school. And since commuters leave after class there is no sense of community, no likelihood of being able to have shared values or sense of mission.

Wherever one goes to college, it is absolutely essential that he becomes a participating member of that community. People who are involved get more out of anything, whether it's college or life, and they are the ones who don't drop out. Every data-gatherer who's done a study has found this to be true. Dr. Alexander Astin, whose work has been the most comprehensive, says flatly that this is a fact of life. And in thirty years on and off campus I can't recall an unhappy or dissatisfied student who was an involved one.

That is not to say that there aren't good and sufficient reasons for wanting to transfer. The student may have made a bad choice, or some special programs or major or ten thousand more people may make another place more alluring. However, transferring to get some specialized major is more often than not a poor idea. Unless a person is an absolute whiz in some field such as physics, which has many specialties, he's going to get all he can carry away in any good college.

When a person wants to transfer from a Grade A college like Grinnell to Boston University, as one girl I know did, she is sacrificing most of the quality of her college for a mess of bigger population pottage. When someone says there's nothing to do or that there's no social life it usually means she hasn't made any effort and hasn't gotten involved. Also, if she says that everyone knows too much about you in a small college, she is missing the point. Or she may want something less troublesome than an education.

Lack of involvement is the reason commuter and part-time students as a group get so much less out of college. They're not a part of the family; they just come to class and go home. Usually there are no meeting places or activities especially for them. And since they're not around for the regular campus activities and cultural or social events, they don't have the benefit of the out-of-class contacts that the residential students do. Consequently, they don't get to know their professors or their classmates as well as they could. So it isn't surprising that, living on the fringe, they are much more likely to drop out. Furthermore, they are much less likely to go on to graduate school.

The shortcomings of the commuter student's experience are worth talking about because parents often are tempted to send a son or daughter who hasn't performed well in high school to a nearby community college for a year to prove himself or herself. They say that it's only the first year, after all, and he or she can have the other three away at college. The troubles with this approach are two: One, the freshman year is at least as important as the other three, probably more so. Two, the community college is going to be an extension of high school; just as distracting, with all the same temptations, and in the company of others for most of whom those two years will be the end of the educational line.

Most of the teenagers at community colleges are not much involved, either academically or in college life. It is the mature students for whom the community colleges are a godsend and who tend to get the most out of what they offer. It requires more than the normal endowment of moral fiber for a teenager to make himself work hard under those circumstances. It is a much better bet to have the student start at a residential college; with luck, one where there is a good learning atmosphere. Not only will the residential college be very likely to be more stimulating, but also living with others who have some interest in learning and achieving is more likely to rub off. The most important single everyday influence is a good studious roommate. That kind is a lot more conducive to good habits than one who says "Let's go to a movie" or "Let's go have a beer." Next, obviously, is the kind of group a student associates with.

The perils of bad roommates notwithstanding, it is important that the student live in the dorms if possible. Simply because they're living right there on the grounds and are part of the scene—unlike students living in apartment houses in town, whose attentions are likely to be focused elsewhere—they're much more likely to be involved in two of the requisites of a good experience: a continuing conversation with one's teachers, who, aside from the library, are the learning resources of the place, and a continuing conversation with one's fellow students.

Even though the condition of most dormitory rooms reflects the fact that most teenagers are slobs should not deter parents, however appalled they are. Thirty years ago, their own college rooms were surely just as bad. In the days when coed dorms were still in their infancy, the columnist Art Buchwald visited the college where his youngest daughter was a freshman. I happened to have visited there a couple of weeks earlier, and thought that even given how unkempt most dorm rooms were, those were awful messes.

Speaking at a convocation, Mr. Buchwald said, "I've had a tour of your campus and I've been through your dorms. And after seeing them, it's not sex in the dorms I'm worried about; it's cholera."

Back in 1979, the *Oberlin Review* carried an article by Sally Brown, a Williams student who was spending her junior year there. It is a good way to end this chapter because it adroitly draws some differences between colleges—which both would say are overdrawn—their students, and their involvement, not to mention the author's talent as a writer:

A PLACE TO COME TO

I hate coming to new places. I never went to sleep away at camp; at least that was the rationalization I used freshman year. I had skipped a year and never gone away for the summer, that's why I hated college. How could I hate college? Seven thousand a year and I had the audacity to hate it.

I went to Williams College in Massachusetts, not the one in Virginia. Actually, I still go there. I am what you would call a "visiting student." Why did I come to Oberlin? I know I need a quick, pat reply. You have to remember that it is unusual to spend junior year abroad forty minutes out of Cleveland.

When I first got to Williams I couldn't believe how pretty it was. It was beautiful and the people were really nice. My "junior adviser's" name was Mary. She had on these amazing pants, red courduroys. This is before Fiorucci started selling them.

First we all went to a semiformal banquet. Everybody put on skirts or suits. We went to the gym and heard speeches. Then the kegs. Every floor of every dorm had a keg and unlike Keep Co-op, people finished them. Everybody was amazed at how diverse I was, coming from New York and all. They couldn't believe I had come out alive. Or that I didn't play tennis. At 18 I realized that I was "counterculture." By junior year I was beginning to believe that I was a revolutionary.

I decided to come to Oberlin, to put Williams into perspective, and maybe to see if I actually had some revolutionary potential. I don't. The guy across the hall had the audacity to call me preppie. He said he could picture me as a Madison Avenue executive. What does he know, anyway?

I showed him when my friend George Rivers Wilbanks Jr. came to visit me. He was driving home for break in his new car. He had an Audi but got bored with it. Now he has a baby blue Impala. He calls her Motown.

He stocked the Dennet house beer machine at Williams. He thought this place was WILD. The co-op was UNBELIEVABLE. Riv went to the Disco. Claims he talked to gay men. Even danced with one of them. WOW. They knew he was straight though. They saw him staring at the women, WILD. He didn't like the beer.

Freshmen at Williams live only with freshmen of their own sex. They usually have singles. Freshmen at Oberlin use bathrooms open to all classes and sexes. They always have doubles. Williams has Homecoming Weekend equipped with semiformal dances with a victorious football team. Oberlin has Mayfair and the Harkness Night Club. When Williams men want to score they road trip to Skidmore. Oberlin women are aware of their bodies and go to Wilder to buy specula.

At Oberlin people want to find themselves. At Williams such angst is unheard of. Everybody at Oberlin has lived on a Kibbutz. Everybody at Williams has met a Jew, usually during their freshman year. Williams students have direction. There are markets to be conquered. Oberlin students see contradictions. There are people to be helped. When Williams students cite tradition it usually means the Republican party. When Oberlin students call forth tradition it usually means progressive action. The Williams liberal political club graduated last year. The Oberlin Moderate Caucus has six members.

This is not to say that Oberlin is utopian or that Williams is hellish. They're just different extremes. They produce different stereotypes. In both cases you find closet moderates.

The Williams stereotype is the career-oriented 90th generation American blond haired business type who plays a wicked game of squash.

The Oberlin stereotype is the guilt-ridden, second generation American brown-haired type with no idea of what they will be doing in five years but may be traveling in the interim.

Introspection is key here. In the past few months I've come to terms with more personal problems than I ever knew I had. One thing is good, I know I'm not being selfish when I talk about these things. It's very important to externalize, you know. Also better for eavesdropping, particularly in the Snack Bar. You find more libidos there than any place else on campus, or in Ohio, for that matter.

Yes, I like Oberlin better than Williams. No, I haven't worked as hard but that could be my courses. Yes, the people are wonderful. No, the landscape doesn't inspire me. No, I'm not going to transfer. It would be very complicated and I'd end up having to spend an extra semester in college. Also Williams is a little better for my career interests.

Here are two great schools and two dramatically different impacts. As this little parody illustrates, the good experience may be very different for different people. And that leads us to the next step: select, don't settle.

6
Select;
Don't Settle

The Test Is Not How
Selective but How Suitable.

The process of choosing a college is a revealing test of a person, of his values, goals, aspirations, and his character. True, his high school record has already said a lot about him, but whether he has excellent or mediocre credentials, he still can make crucial college decisions. The test is not how selective but how suitable the college.

In no other country does such a plethora of choices so confuse the issue or encourage so many frivolous decisions with such costly consequences. For several decades, according to an Office of Education study in the late fifties, only four out of ten freshmen were in the same colleges for four years. But a 1987 Department of Education survey of the class of 1972 found the retention rate had shrunk to three in ten. Furthermore, three of the leaving seven didn't even return for the sophomore year.

There is a lot of chaff to sift through because the higher education establishment was profligately overbuilt in the long spending spree touched off at the end of World War II by the GI Bill of Rights. Until inflation and the Reagan cutbacks, education was not just a growth industry, it was a boom, and as *Washington Post* critic Jonathan Yardley observed, every locality that could muster enough legislative clout got a branch campus of the state university and then demanded the legislature decree it a "university." The teachers' colleges, their alumni, and local business interests likewise demanded and got the same phony status conferred upon their normal schools.

Now, as the *Chronicle of Higher Education* has reported, state after state has tried to close down some of these useless, ersatz universities, and with one exception in South Dakota, to no avail. And there the closing has brought a flurry of lawsuits. In Texas, when the closing of Sul Ross State University, a place of twenty-three hundred students in a town of five thousand, was proposed, the legislative committee was snowed with seventy thousand letters of protest and one thousand people traveled four hundred miles to Austin to do battle for the local economy. Naturally, Sul Ross "university" lives on. Similarly, when Connecticut tried to shut the two-hundred-student university branch at Torrington, the area's legislative representatives kept it alive under another name. Colorado's legislature even limits enrollment at the main university campus at Boulder so as to force-feed the parochial branch campuses, which the local voters demand.

Since 80 percent of America's college students are in public institutions, the double cheating of students and taxpayers is on a vast scale. Those places whose main reason for being is political aren't likely to have commitments to quality, so a student and his parents would be foolish not to do some hard-nosed on-site consumer research and to check the value of the institution's degree in the business and academic worlds.

How Does One Spot Such a Place?

If the student body is predominantly in-state and a sizable percentage of students leaves on weekends, or worse, if it's commuter, and if in addition most of the degrees are in vocational programs such as teacher education or business, it is not likely to have any sense of community or to be a community of learning.

Teacher education programs are held in such contempt in the academic world that there has been pressure to abandon them in favor of giving teachers a real education. If the institution is devoted to teacher certification and other job-training programs, the concern is probably credentialing.

Naturally, such places are not the best bets for getting into graduate or professional schools. Also, to an out-of-state student they probably would seem provincial. Nearly every state has at least one such public institution. They debase the currency of higher education because they purport to provide entry into the company of educated people.

At a party a few years ago, when I asked the chairman of the physics department at Towson State in Maryland, an institution with ten thousand undergraduates, how many majors he had, he replied, "I've never had a physics major." And he had been there ten years. Though he subsequently became a top administrator, he forsook such barren toil for the investment business's rewards.

The lesson for the buyer is clear. A place that hasn't had a physics major in ten years probably hasn't had much intellectual life of any kind. Even with the stimulus of majors, it may be difficult for a faculty member in a place with no sense of mission to be an inspiring teacher. And now that higher education is no longer a growth industry, many a faculty member who thought an appointment at State College would be just one quick step up the ladder to a better place has found himself stuck and lucky to have a job. It often is a double whammy because the professor's spouse is probably a smart and capable person who may have sacrificed a job or career of his or her own for what they both thought would be a brief stop. Now they're in a town that may not offer much beside a local industry or two, farms, and the university. The students get the benefit of better professors than they might otherwise have, but the tingle is likely to be missing.

What About the State Universities?

With some exceptions in Alabama, California, Florida, Maryland, New York, Ohio, Virginia, and Washington, to be discussed later, the main campuses of the state universities have most of the good faculty and the best programs. They also get bad marks as undergraduate colleges. Indeed, simply put, unless one gets in the honors program, the undergraduate is likely to be cheated. The University of Wisconsin, for example, which has lots of pizzazz and is one of the world's most distinguished universities and has had more than its share of faculty Nobel laureates, leaves nearly three quarters of the freshmen and sophomore instruction to graduate assistants. And much of the rest is in large lecture sections. However, a top student who gets in the peerless Honors Program will be in mostly small classes with other students who are there to learn and will be taught by the best faculty members. The honors programs there and elsewhere are attempts to provide for a very select few the same quality provided for everyone at a good undergraduate college, or, as they say, "quality within the context of quantity."

But the University Boasts of Its Famous Scholars.

The famous scholar probably has only glancing contact with undergraduates. The scholar's principal interests are where the professional rewards are, in research and publishing. As for what teaching they do, they much prefer the Ph.D. candidates who are not only nearer their level, but who can also serve as research assistants. If any documentation were needed, it was provided by Dr. Boyer's previously mentioned book, *College.* He and his team found that in the research universities 25 percent of the faculty did no teaching at all, 35 percent taught only one to four hours a week, and another 30 percent taught only five to ten hours. So 90 percent of the faculty did less teaching than the twelve to fourteen hours a week considered a normal load in many colleges.

In sharp contrast, only 3 percent of the liberal arts college faculty did no teaching, and only 13 percent taught as little as four hours.

And in the critical area of advising students—an area where even the best colleges sometimes fall flat on their faces—Dr. Boyer's team found "almost without exception" that faculty at large institutions are less actively involved, although they still spend time informally with students, especially those who have selected their majors. Only 9 percent of the students they talked to at liberal arts colleges felt they were treated like numbers, whereas 62 percent at the research universities did. They also found that at the liberal arts colleges 75 percent of the students asked felt that professors took an interest in their academic progress. For all institutions the figure was 59 percent.

A professor leaving academia wrote in a *Chronicle of Higher Education* article that a nameless University of California professor said, "The sight of an undergraduate makes me sick." The author went on to write that once "I looked forward to the day when I too could say that." It's an attitude that goes with the territory.

Is a Small- or Medium-Size University Better?

Unfortunately, the problem isn't a matter of size. Johns Hopkins, with an enrollment of thirty-one hundred, is no larger than some colleges, but great as it is, undergraduates suffer from the research university condition. Science majors are likely to find themselves in large classes even as seniors, although Hopkins advertises a ten to one student-faculty ratio and a faculty studded with famous scholars.

Students in the less crowded humanities may have the kind of mixed experience one of my young friends has had. An English major, she was euphoric her first semester to be half the class with a renowned scholar, and one with whom the two could have a discussion, not just get a lecture from. But too often it was the case of a scholar begrudging three hours of his valuable time each week to lecture to undergraduates. When I told a former faculty member that the student had found so many of her instructors indifferent to undergraduates, he retorted, "They're not indifferent; they're hostile!" Another client, a biology major, said he'd had no more than five minutes of his adviser's time in three years. He should have been more aggressive, but at a good small college such a situation would have been most unlikely. The undergraduate is its only product.

Bigger Is Not Better.

While the popular belief is that bigger is better and therefore a university must be better than a small college, the big university faculty members and administrators know that bigger is likely to be inferior. So many of them send their own children to undergraduate colleges that it has sometimes been a political embarrassment in trying to convince Congress that the big places should get most or all of the Federal funds. A former president of the University of Minnesota sent his son to Carleton; two vice presidents of MIT have sent their children to Carleton and to Wooster. Many years ago when a young client asked about the University of Maryland after we had discussed several colleges, I gave him a spate of reasons why not: big classes, graduate-assistant teaching, inability to get any help in some departments, much less be able to discuss things with teachers, an entire grade depending often on one or two multiple-choice tests, and an anti-intellectual atmosphere too concerned with credentials. When they were ready to leave, I said to the father, "Oh, I forgot to ask what you do." He replied, "I'm on the faculty at Maryland, but I agree with everything you said."

Another time, when the daughter of a Hopkins professor asked me about that school, I said, "Your father's going to hit me, but if you were going to be a science major at Hopkins, which is preeminent in that field, you'd be in amphitheater-size classes your senior year, but if you were going to be an art history, English lit, or political science major, after your fresh-

man year you'd have many of the advantages of a good small
college: small classes, some contact with the professors, and
maybe even make friends with them." "I'll buy that," he said.
And to a now-famous educator who because of his present role
might be red-faced if identified, but then a University of Pennsylvania administrator, I once said that just about every big
university is a gyp joint for the undergraduate, "including
yours." He looked a bit startled, grinned, and said, "That's
right."

A dentist friend and his wife persuaded their son to transfer
from Washington University to the University of Wisconsin because it was bigger, had more facilities, and they thought a
better entrée to medical school. It didn't work that way. He was
rejected at every medical school he applied to, including Wisconsin. Had he stayed at Washington University, the medical
school admissions director there told me they'd have accepted
him because, as one of their own, he'd have had some pref-
erence as a known product, with recommendations from known
professors. At Wisconsin, he was just another of the more than
twenty-six hundred qualified out-of-state applicants. After much
anguished searching, he found a last-gasp acceptance.

A mother, who like her husband, is a University of Chicago
graduate, wrote me that given their two daughters' experiences
at Carleton and at Kenyon, "we have become strong supporters
of the good small liberal arts college." One girl had tried the
University of Florida for a year, and among other things she
offered a universal truth when she said, "They may have two
thousand courses, but try to get in one. You're bound to get
screwed." And two Phi Beta Kappa alumni of the University of
North Carolina became disenchanted after their twins' freshman
year there. Said the mother, "They don't keep their promises
in any respect to parents. They [the twins] have no class
courses, no teaching at all, just TV screens. Just sign up for
the exams when they've finished the assignments."

Occasionally I have one or two university professors and
their children as clients and the parents invariably prefer the

small college. They know that the renowned scholar, if he is a performer on a stage rather than a mentor in a dialogue, is not going to affect their son or daughter much because education is a discourse.

The student council president at Vassar told me he picked it over Brown when he saw how much larger Brown's classes were. Only the honors programs at Michigan or Wisconsin can compare with the quality of instruction and close personal contact between teacher and student at colleges in their states such as Kalamazoo, Beloit, or Lawrence.

What Are the Public Academic Bargains?

The public institutions that are the real academic bargains are the relatively few undergraduate ones. In Alabama, the University of Montevallo, with twenty-eight hundred students, has the advantages of a good private college at a fraction of the cost. In California, the excellent cluster college campuses of the University of California at Santa Cruz and San Diego are groups of small colleges on enormous campuses of twelve hundred and two thousand acres. San Diego has four colleges: Revelle, designed to give a student exposure to all branches of learning; Muir, where the student assumes some responsibility for planning his own program and has considerable freedom of choice; Third College, whose central concern is social and societal problems; and Warren, a liberal arts school that is career-oriented. San Diego is outstanding in the sciences, computer science, and engineering. Santa Cruz has eight small residential colleges and was founded to offer high quality undergraduate work with close student-faculty relations and an innovative approach.

For the able student who wants to do honors work and, unlike most teenagers, can accept responsibility for working on his own, New College of the University of South Florida offers a different kind of choice. Unlike St. John's College in Annapolis or Santa Fe, where the curriculum is fixed, or Reed where there is a core of required courses, the four hundred students at New College make contracts for what they propose to do and there are no required courses. There are, however, three independent study projects, a senior thesis, and an oral defense of it before a faculty panel.

In Maryland, in the city where, in 1634, the ships the *Ark* and the *Dove* landed with the state's first settlers, St. Mary's College gives one thousand fortunate students a good college experience in a water resort setting, at a third of the cost of a private college. But with out-of-state enrollment at only 15 percent, the weekend exodus is heavy.

For countless New Yorkers and others with good grades who don't want to or don't get into an Ivy League school, that state offers in Harpur College, the liberal arts component of the State University at Binghamton, something as good or better. In most other states, a low-cost public institution of such high quality for the undergraduate would make the competition tough for the good private colleges. But since New York and New England didn't even make a start toward providing public higher education until the middle of this century, the natives have tended to think of anything public as second rate—an attitude that would be incomprehensible to college-seekers in California, Michigan, North Carolina, Virginia, or Wisconsin, for example.

Binghamton has always been the unit in the state system committed to the liberal arts, although it has schools of nursing, management, engineering, and professional education. And although it has three thousand graduate as well as ninety-five hundred undergraduate students, there is a strong commitment to teaching and to faculty-student contact, and its residential colleges have faculty masters as well as faculty fellows assigned to each. Until recently, fewer than 5 percent of the students came from outside New York. Now, as the result of a program to increase diversity, the figure has climbed to 9 percent, and twenty-three states are represented.

Far larger, with about fourteen thousand students, Miami University in Oxford, Ohio, has few graduate assistants and less such teaching than any other public institution in the state, and as an undergraduate school it is head and shoulders above any of them. Its freshman class has a pre–school orientation week in which the new students and teachers get acquainted, which contributes to a sense of community and a personality. A beautiful campus and high standards have always made it an attractive alternative to an Ivy League school. And in recent years it has become nearly as selective as one for an out-of-stater.

Virginia has two public bargains: William and Mary and Mary Washington. William and Mary, where Phi Beta Kappa was founded, used to be where, a few decades back, academic ne'er-do-wells from the North relaxed in sleepy Williamsburg. Now it is so selective that only very good students have a chance of getting in. And since the school can have only 30 percent out-of-state students, it is more selective than most of the Ivies for the non-Virginian, and nearly so for the natives, for whom, like the University in Charlottesville, it is a status symbol. The students are good, faculty members testify, but not venturesome or challenging; they reflect a conservative state.

Mary Washington in Fredericksburg, a female satellite of the University of Virginia before the university went coed, is much less selective, has about six hundred men and eighteen hundred women, 80 percent of whom are Virginians, which means not much diversity, a heavy weekend exodus, and a comfortable, conventional atmosphere.

Evergreen State College in Olympia, Washington, is an outstanding academic bargain, but it is as untraditional as Antioch or Hampshire or St. John's or Deep Springs or New because it requires a commitment to learning that puts the monkey on the student's back. And most teenagers aren't ready for this. The first year, groups of sixty to one hundred students are team-taught by three to five faculty members in an interdisciplinary approach to a central theme. For more advanced work, a student may make an individual or a group contract for self-designed programs negotiated by faculty member and student.

There are no grades, but rather faculty evaluations, and there are student evaluations of faculty as well.

Where to Look for Most of the Bargains.

Most of the academic bargains are in the nearly nine hundred private undergraduate colleges (some of which call themselves universities). These are the ones likely to have an impact on a person's life and that are usually much easier to get into than the Ivies.

A Lot of These Colleges Are Church-Related. Do They Indoctrinate?

Rarely is this a concern. While virtually every private college started life church-related, most such ties today are tenuous if they exist at all. Some few fundamentalist colleges, such as Liberty or Oral Roberts, have rigid rules of conduct and beliefs, or may, like Gordon College in Massachusetts, require that an applicant declare Christ as his savior, but they are the exceptions. The Methodist and Presbyterian colleges that a few decades ago had curfews for women—and some even for men—now have coed dorms and may sell beer in the student unions. Catholic colleges still require religion courses but may have Jews and Protestants in the theology departments. Academically, a wind has been blowing through the Catholic colleges but they still tend to be homogeneous. Georgetown, now a "hot" college, has 40 percent non-Catholic students, but most of the other big-name Catholic schools like Notre Dame, Boston College, Holy Cross, or Villanova are more homogeneous with 80 to 90 percent Catholics. A student at Holy Cross, trying to sum it up for a *Time* reporter, said, "We're all white Anglo-Saxon Protestants here."

What Good Are Liberal Arts Colleges for My Career Needs?

Until the shifting sands of a developing service economy revived interest in them, parents and students too often perceived the "liberal arts" as vague, unfocused, pointing to no career, and therefore impractical. Too many still do, and the next time the job market gets discouraging, parents again will want their college students to have specific job goals in mind, no matter what the evidence that that's not the payoff. If, after four expensive years of college, stories of Joe and Jane waiting tables or driving a cab with no idea of what they want to do are on every neighbor's clucking tongue, parents will feel they have a social disease. And rising college costs will aggravate their condition. They will want a college that has a menu of suitable vocational programs—advertising, business, law, or whatever —that they envision as being hooked securely into the market for a first job.

In most cases, they could not be more wrong, for two reasons. The first, a reflection of the swiftness of change in our economy, is an upheaval in the ways people earn their living. Most of the fast-growing list of careers in the occupational directories, like most of the wonder drugs on the pharmacists' shelves, weren't there before World War II, which indicates the manpower experts have been pretty good prophets. They have been saying for years that because of the changing nature of and the fast-growing list of kinds of work, today's students are likely to have three or four different careers or branches off a main stem. And what's more, a lot of those careers have yet to come into existence.

It follows that the supposed security of a currently profitable role in the American establishment in a stable world is diminishing. Increasingly, new opportunities are springing up that only the prepared brain can envision and exploit. That wonderful quality of serendipity, often mistaken for luck, opens to the enlightened person new ways to use his talents and interests in satisfying pursuits. The specialist, wearing the blinders of his training, may be unable to envision and exploit new opportunities. He is the more likely candidate for what Thoreau called a life of quiet desperation.

The second reason parents are wrong is that people, as well as their options, change and grow. Hardly anyone has a crystal ball clear enough to divine what's going to appeal to him fifteen years hence. And the parents are themselves walking proofs that their worry about their son or daughter getting that first job is groundless. Just as their adult successes screen from their memories their own teenage uncertainties and shortcomings, so they cannot understand why their eighteen-year-olds don't know what they want to do and get about the business of doing it. But the kids are not failures and the parents need not be ashamed; it's a normal situation. The parents were probably in the same boat a generation earlier.

To test that belief, when the job market became discouraging in the late seventies I started asking an additional biographical question of all the fathers and mothers who came to my office; namely, what their original college majors had been as freshmen. I knew what the answers would be. In 1970, the Carnegie Corporation had funded a study to find out whether a college major was a reliable indicator of a person's future vocation. It was not.

In only three fields—engineering, teacher education, and business administration—did the majority remain true to their choices. Fifteen years out of college, 75 to 96 percent of the men in all the other fields, whether the humanities, arts, social sciences, sciences, or mathematics, had forsaken their original interests. Women proved even more changeable. And there are some important caveats to come on those fields where people tended to stay.

What I've found has been strikingly similar. Of about 2,000 individuals, only 208 have stayed in the fields which they originally chose as majors. Most are in careers not even remotely

related. The bulk of the faithful are women who had planned
to be teachers, because for many years a teaching certificate
guaranteed a job.

Not only have nine out of ten of these parents changed careers, but a good many have made two or three changes. One
father who had majored in economics in preparation for taking
over the family furniture business tired of that and finally yielded
to a long-held urge to have his own kennel. He was happy in
that until a psychologist friend took him along on a visit to a
state institution. The next day he telephoned to ask if he could
go back to school and get a Master of Social Work degree, the
experience had so fired him up. He did and he now has an
additional role: social worker.

Another father shifted from psychology to owning a group
of car washes and selling equipment for them, and still another
moved from an engineering degree to one in law and a career
in the Justice Department. Another apostate engineer became
an administrative law judge. A mother who was a fine arts major
now heads special education for a block of suburban schools.

A successful industrial realty developer had first tried chemistry and then social relations at Harvard. A management con-
sultant got as far as a master's degree in physics before finding
his true love. A fledgling geologist who is a corporate official
was a presidential environment adviser.

The owner of a popular Baltimore restaurant is a registered
pharmacist, while the head of a coffee-shop chain there is a
German literature major. Another German lit major shifted in
graduate school to political science and economics and became a Central Intelligence Agency economist. A Washington
investment firm and an insurance brokerage firm are owned,
respectively, by the holder of a master's in geography and a
science major.

A Hopkins faculty member's doctorate in political science
was a jump from his original major, business, while a former
political scientist now runs a travel agency in Baltimore.

English literature majors are scattered all over the employment scene twenty years out of college and in roles worlds removed from their major. One is a budget official at the National Institutes of Health; another switched to anthropology and directs a study of metropolitan problems for this same agency of many concerns. A third was director of several major programs in what was the Department of Health, Education and Welfare. A high official of the Organization of American States thought philosophy was his field until he fell for law and then for international relations.

The parents who are still doing something stemming from their undergraduate interests tend to be doctors (but some were music, art history, and sociology majors), accountants, college faculty members, schoolteachers, businessmen, and engineers. And many of the last are no longer in engineering; they're in management dealing with people. One of the faithful few, however, a successful builder and developer, says of his business administration major at Rutgers, "It was absolutely useless!"

And some of those who never complete a major also find happiness, like a CIA official who says he was tossed out of a most prestigious school.

It's hardly surprising then that studies consistently show that:

- Two thirds of the college students change their career plans at least once, often twice, in those four years.
- Most graduates change jobs at least once in the first five years after college, even on the graduate level. Harvard found it happens even to its Master of Business Administration alumni.
- Only 30 percent of those who start in engineering graduate, chiefly because it does demand an early commitment.
- Two thirds of the administrators in business did not major in that field.

The teaching certificate has lost its gilt edge, partly because women now have the same broad array of career opportunities as men and are crowding the men in graduate and professional schools.

Because no one knows how the fabric of his or her life will be woven and thus what may turn out to be relevant, learning is negative as well as positive. It may be just as important to discover after a semester or a year on the wrong track that one doesn't really like engineering or psychology as it is to find that one's real love is art history or economics. The chemists say that nothing ever ceases to exist. In education it is hard to think of any experience that is wasted—even a dead end—if it helps a person find out who he is.

The knowledge may come in handy in some wholly unexpected way. A young woman who graduated from Michigan with a degree in biology said that on cap and gown day she asked herself, "Why did I do this? I don't want to teach and I'm not interested in being a research scientist." So she went back and got a Master of Business Administration degree. The combination qualified her for what was then a new kind of job: figuring out, in the Environmental Protection Agency, the environmental impact of a proposed commercial or industrial installation.

The Best Plan: Prepare to Cope.

A teenager planning for college and a parent thinking of how he's going to pay for it often can't see why a liberal education is a better investment than a specialized one because the return as measured by first-job prospects seems so chancy. Like the Federal Reserve Board's tightening or loosening of the money supply, the effects of a real education take a while to show up. The liberal arts graduate quite often has more trouble finding his first job than does the engineer, accountant, or other specialist. But he winds up better satisfied and—because he has learned to think, to adapt, and to communicate—being the specialist's boss. So, making decisions aimed at a first job is like assuming the first-inning score is going to be the final one. That kind of thinking can damage peoples' lives.

So What Is the Message?

The message is that a good selecting job deserves as much research and hard thinking as a term paper and will do more for you.

Assuming that you have done the work in Chapter 3 and have an idea of why you're going and what you want, you must then read, read, read. There's no getting away from the pick-and-shovel work. Here are some things to keep in mind:

1. Settle on your priorities and hold to them.

Don't get mired in irrelevancies. Don't worry about the proximity of ski slopes or beaches or geography or climate. Don't fall victim to the instant gratification impulse. The fun items will be plentiful enough on occasional weekends, vacations, or after college. Besides, there'll be plenty of playtime on campus, not to mention off-campus study programs in this country and abroad. College is no convent; indeed, the trouble is not too few temptations but too many.

2. Reread the Twenty Myths, with particular attention to Three, Five, Six, and Nine.

Doing this may help keep you on track if you think, like so many high school seniors, that you need to be in or near a city, or that your college must have an enrollment of "at least five thousand," as so many specify. Or you may think there's some magic in geography, or that you're afraid your friends—whom you probably won't even know five years hence—may not have heard of it.

These three considerations are the nearly universal irrelevancies I try to disabuse clients of. And if many of them who went to colleges that were (a) not near a city, (b) much smaller than five thousand, and (c) had little name recognition had been dissatisfied, I would long since have been in some other line of work.

Doing that reading may reassure you of good company, plenty of competition, and as lively a life outside of class as you want. And if it leads you to consider schools you otherwise wouldn't have, it may prove a good lifetime investment.

3. Don't rule out a college because you don't like that state.

For example, at the mention of West Virginia, parents' eyes often glaze over. One year it happened with four families. All four visited the colleges discussed and all four students went. One of the fathers on his return called to say, "West Virginia Wesleyan is a fabulous place!" Similarly, a mother who had been apprehensive about Kansas jubilantly reported, "Kansas City is a wonderful place!" What's more, her son got good enough grades at Park College to get into medical school, something he couldn't have done at the University of Maryland.

A well-to-do Baltimore mother whose reservations about Davis and Elkins were geographical wrote four years later to say how much that college had done for her son's personal and mental development.

Once, after I'd suggested some Midwest colleges for a bright girl with middling grades, her Harvard College, Harvard Law father demanded, "Why are all those schools in Iowa?" "Because," I answered, "they're better than the selective ones in the East she can't get into."

4. Cast off home-state shackles in reaching your decision.

This can be just as important as letting a geographical prejudice rule out a college. A lot of people who otherwise use their noggins think they can and will come home more often if they go to a college in-state because it will be handier. I asked a girl who'd gone to a college in southwest Virginia for this reason how many times she'd come home to Alexandria—other than holidays—in two years. "None," she said. And if she had, a lot of closer places in other states, or farther away but handier to airports, would have made for easier traveling. All she had done was to narrow her options. Besides, if one's program is sufficiently demanding, it's going to require some time in the library most weekends. And with so many on-campus activities, why would you want to leave?

5. Don't feel limited by finances to the nearest or cheapest place.

If the family income is really that low, you will qualify for financial aid and it literally may be cheaper to go away to an expensive private college than live at home and go to a free public one. More than one financial aid officer has said too many parents just assume they're not eligible for aid and don't ask. Some states, however, give aid grants for use only in that state.

6. Don't be blinded by offers of an athletic scholarship.

If the Federal Trade Commission ever started prosecuting the frauds in this area, there'd be a lot of presidents as well as coaches under indictment. [Clemson's president resigned when the board of trustees refused to let him clean up things there, which gives a clue to the Clemson ethos.] The scholarship may be revoked if you don't make the team or if you get hurt. And as Dr. Jan Kemp, who was fired by the University of Georgia for fighting for an honest athletic tutoring program, sued and won back her job and a $1 million damage award, said, "It's still the plantation system, but the slaves are scoring touchdowns instead of picking cotton, and if they don't produce, they can't live in the big house."

But more important, this is making a central decision for the wrong reason. One of my young friends who had decided the Great Books program at St. John's College was just the thing for him, went to the University of Virginia when offered a track scholarship. He stayed one semester and transferred to St. John's. He'd got his priorities back in order.

The Other Side of the Coin: Things to Do

1. Step your choices down; don't make them all on one level, or top and bottom.

Too many people make the mistake of trying for two or three at the top of their lists and then dropping way down in quality or desirability to schools that are clearly safe, only because they are safe. In so doing, one sacrifices quality and some of the good he should get from college. If he had taken the trouble to find out about more colleges—ones he'd never heard of—he'd have profited happily. And the college he'd not known about before might prove better than the original choice.

2. Pick a school because you like its ethos, its atmosphere, what it stands for, because it fits you, not because you've heard it has a good department in the subject you plan to major in. You may well change your major; most people do.

If it's an undergraduate college, almost any department is going to offer a lot more than you're going to be able to take away in four years. Teenagers are misled by this quality-of-department talk. Faculty Ph.D.'s are journeymen who've attained the doctoral level by negotiating the same rigorous course, and in this age of a soft academic market any college that doesn't have qualified faculty hasn't tried, or has a lot of tenured faculty who can't be fired.

The important thing is whether they are good teachers whose primary interest is in teaching and students rather than research. The publishing scholar in the university may not give undergraduates the time of day.

Remember, too, that the professor who has gotten to know you can write a far more cogent and persuasive recommendation than the one to whom you may be a face in the lecture hall, if that.

3. Pick the college that looks like it will be the most demanding one you can get into.

This may not be the most selective one; indeed, you may be surprised at how much harder you'll have to work at some college that accepts most of its applicants than at some very selective ones. The college that does something for you is the one that challenges you; otherwise, you're wasting your time.

4. Use the directories to get some indicators, such as the percentage that goes on to graduate study in what fields, what percentage leaves campus on weekends, what the most popular majors are, whether it's residential or commuter.

5. Use the telephone to ask questions of admissions and faculty people about how much time students spend studying, how many pages they read a night, or whatever else may concern you. Consult the catalogs for faculty and staff names. The librarian is a good one to try to ask for help. Most faculty members will level with you. Call the student newspaper or any student organization you can locate. This is worth the effort and can lead to a visit or supplement one.

Alumni in your area are a good source of information; in fact, as you'll see in Chapter 14, one of them may interview you if you apply. Now is a good time to get in the first lick and make him be the subject. The school will probably give you the names of nearby alums who are willing to talk to students.

If You Are Committed to a Big School

Be as choosy as you can. Try to get into an honors program for the top students, or into a residential college, or any other select, small-group program that seems suitable to you. Even without meeting the required grade point average, it may be possible to petition to get into individual honors classes. They have the better teachers, better, more involved students, and smaller classes. They are more demanding and, as a consequence, more stimulating. And besides doing you more good, they are likely to impress a prospective employer. The residential or other small-group programs will give a sense of community within the big university and perhaps a lot more contact with professors than the general school population has.

Pick the least vocationally oriented program you can. After the freshman year at least, there's likely to be more contact with teachers, smaller classes, more learning, and less training.

Also, you will learn more philosophy from a first-rate teacher in economics than a second-rate one in philosophy, so look for the best teachers and the toughest ones, not the popular, easy-grading lecturers. The good ones are those who have high expectations of their students as well as of themselves. On every faculty in the land, there are clunks and there are people who can make a difference in your life. Seek them out.

Remember that as important as selecting the right college is, the attitude with which you go is even more important. Indeed, attitude is 95 percent of the battle, in college or anywhere else.

7
Sample and Test the Merchandise

Whan that Aprille with his shoures soote
The droghte of Marche hath perced to the roote,
And bathed every veyne in swich licour
Of which vertu engendered is the flour; . . .
Than longen folk to goon on pilgrimages . . .
Prologue, *The Canterbury Tales*

Chaucer's *Canterbury Tales* depicted one of medieval England's great spring events, the salvation-seeking pilgrimages to the shrine of the martyred Saint Thomas à Becket. Were Chaucer alive today and chronicling America's spring and summer pilgrimages of college-seekers, he'd find them far more numerous, much more middle class than motley, and the caravans tiny: usually two parents and a teenager or two. And rather than a common holy place, each little band would be seeking out three or four of its own: the campuses from which to pick the teenager's college of choice.

Should he choose to compare the efficacy of the medieval and the modern journeys, Chaucer would be compelled to give the nod to those who put their faith in the martyr. They at least

97

lived thereafter in hope, whereas today's pilgrims often find their hopes turning to dross. This is partly because their pilgrimages are made at the wrong time, in the wrong way, and by the wrong folk. Also, they are looking at the physical trappings, possibly attending spring rites such as graduations that have little relevance to the quest, and more than likely missing the heart of the matter while assessing the real estate.

This is one of many reasons why most college choices fail to last and why only about three of every ten freshmen are in the same colleges four years later.

This chapter will tell you in detail how to be a smart pilgrim, and will list a lot of questions you should ask that will tell you whether a particular college would be a good choice for you.

In an ideal world of college-choosing, the pilgrim should go alone, on a school day, and spend a working day and a night doing a well-prepared, hard-nosed inquiry into the nature of the place and its inhabitants.

That should come after he has done these three things:

—One, read the catalog to see what the graduation requirements consist of and what special programs and off-campus experiences are offered, and whether the catalog gives any hint of what the four years there might do for one. This is important because in many places, especially many large public universities, it is not only possible but the easiest thing in the world to get a degree without ever getting anything faintly resembling an education. And that is what happens to most.

—Two, completed a probing self-assessment, as discussed in Chapter 3, plus a draft or two of a personal statement, so you'll be better able to talk about yourself.

—Three, made a list of Ralph Nader–like questions to ask about what kinds of experiences others are having there. These should be things that are important to you, the pilgrim, however odd they might seem to someone else. And the questions may well change after the experience gained in the first visit. A sample list of questions will be given later on.

A parent may have objections to such a rigorous visiting

procedure: "It takes a lot of work; my seventeen-year-old is too young to go alone, and besides, I want to go along." True, it is a lot of work, but very little compared to the importance of the project. The teenager won't be too young to go next fall; why is he now? The parents can and probably should go, but on condition they and the student part company at the campus gate. They can compare notes later. Going with a friend is a no-no for the same reason: the student may talk to the parents or friend instead of asking questions.

College costs somewhere between a Cadillac at a public institution and a top-of-the-line Mercedes at a private one, and it can have a profound influence on the quality of a person's life. So why choose one without inspecting the merchandise rather than its packaging, and without doing some comparison shopping?

A random example of what may happen otherwise—and it's one of a countless number of examples occurring at other institutions—is that of a suburban Washington boy and his father who had made only a summer visit to the University of Southern California the previous year. When they came to me the father said, "Very clear representations were made to us that although this was a large university, classes were small, there was much personal contact, and plenty of individual counseling. What my son found was a mass-production mill of big classes, unavailable professors, easy courses, and rampant cheating." The son, who had made the Dean's List, transferred to Claremont McKenna, a Grade A college with an enrollment of nine hundred, but only after doing the working-day investigation he should have done at USC. His efforts really found for him the things the USC official had claimed.

Most colleges, but not often the universities, are happy to put visitors up overnight in the dorms and give them cafeteria passes. Some of the universities give group campus tours, which are of little value for probing the character of the place. A call to the admissions office will be sufficient to arrange a visit, and the person making the arrangements will probably ask what classes the visitor would like to attend, and whether an interview is desired.

The anxiety about the interview is great but vastly overdone. At few places and in few cases is it decisive or even very important, as the chapter on that subject points out. What the applicant says in his or her written application and what the objective data on that record say about him or her are the critical elements. Besides, only a small fraction of applicants get to campuses for interviews.

If the number of school days available for visiting is much restricted, try traveling on a Sunday, going to classes Monday, and getting back to high school for Tuesday classes. Or, travel Thursday afternoon, go to classes on Friday, and have the weekend to extend the visit if needed. The number of classes on Friday afternoon may be limited, however.

It is important to go as a customer, not as a supplicant. In that role, don't buy everything the college may tell you. They're all marketing their wares; their sales pitches may not cover the things that are important to you and may need to be put in perspective or even taken with more than a grain of salt. Furthermore, even if a person has done some self-examination, he may not fully realize at first look or hearing what things really will be important to him. It takes questioning to make the comparisons and the contrasts clear.

That means having the time to spend a day and a night, going to a few classes, eating in the cafeteria, and sleeping in the dorm. This gives the time to ask questions and to think of follow-ups, and the leisure to chat with students and faculty. Weekend visits aren't likely to produce anywhere near the same results as a visit on a working day.

Reactions to a visit may be as much visceral as cerebral, as are the major decisions of life, but the viscera will operate more truly if the brain is informed. Conclusions shouldn't be drawn on the basis of one or two opinions or on the impression made by the interviewer or the campus guide. For example, a good New England college alienated at least one girl's family because the student showing them around carried a can of beer, a sin he probably did not commit again. Or the campus tour guide may take the visitors past the library and into the student union and its video games, pinball machines, and snack bars. While a tour guide enthusiastic about the wrong things is at the very least a bad mark against the way the admissions office is run and should be taken seriously, it doesn't in itself necessarily disqualify the college.

Since in this rich country anyone can get into a college that can challenge him, whatever his academic abilities, the visitor should assume the role of probing consumer. There's no risk; there are so many good colleges of all kinds that if one school says no, at least one other will say yes. It may be beyond fantasy to expect a high school senior visiting Harvard or Stanford, for instance, to put on such confident armor but it is nonetheless true.

College-arranged visiting days for captive groups of prospects are what in pre-glasnost days were called Russian tours; they permit the college to put its best foot forward without permitting too-close scrutiny. Similarly, college nights and college fairs are circuses for selling the colleges. They do little or nothing to sort things out, even though the fair is full of sales managers.

Since every college visitor isn't looking for the same thing, the same questions won't work for everyone, but there are plenty of clues to discovering whether a school is a good and comfortable fit. The important thing is to ask the questions that deal with your particular needs. The college may be right for a friend or it may be one that's popular in your high school. But maybe your friend likes vanilla and you don't. Even less relevant is the college's popularity with other members of the senior class. The seniors at another school will, in their wisdom, be favoring a different college. At almost any suburban high school a large chunk of the class will apply to the same school, not because it offers a fine education but because it's peer-approved. Considering that the chances are at least a hundred to one that the paths and interests of high school friends will scatter them even in their first year of college, today's peer approval will turn out to be empty tomorrow, leaving some regrets.

To be a smart customer, make overnight visits to at least a couple of colleges if possible, for comparison's sake, and follow a plan like this:

Things to Do

1. Talk to a couple of dozen students and a few faculty members. This provides a better sample and can tell you whether a bad impression is a fluke or characteristic. The praise or the gripe that is out of the pattern can be put in perspective and you're in less danger of kissing off a good place or buying a pig in a poke. Don't spend your time with just one or two people.

2. Go to at least two classes. A typical freshman class, especially if it's a required general education course, and perhaps an upper division class in your area of interest are useful ones.

3. Eat in the cafeteria. That's the place where you'll get more answers to more questions than almost anywhere else. And sit at a big table where six or eight kids are sitting; that way you'll get a lot of responses to your questions.

4. Visit the faculty offices; knock on some doors and ask questions. This is where you'll get a slant on the students and answers you might not get anywhere else.

5. Visit the bookstore. Fifteen minutes here will tell you a lot about the character of the school. If it has virtually all textbooks with little or nothing for secondary reading or independent study and no general literature but lots of beer mugs, ashtrays, glasses, and pennants with the college seal it may indicate a lot of college spirit but not much intellectual orientation. But if it has inexpensive classical music and art prints and a wide range of good books, that's a very good sign.

6. Visit the newspaper and, if there is one, the radio station.

Here are people who ought to have their fingers on the pulse of the place.

7. Visit the student government office for the same reason.

8. Investigate the library and its use.

9. Have an admissions interview if the college wants it or if you have questions you want to ask, such as, would I be accepted?

10. Spend a night in the dorm. This means a longer, less hurried visit and a chance to think about what you've learned and whether you need to ask some follow-up questions in the morning.

Questions to Ask of Students and of Yourself

• What are the chief gripes of people around here? This is a good opener that gets things going. When I asked a former client, a sophomore, his response was, "It's awfully hard to be humble at Amherst." But usually this question gives some revealing clues and suggestions for further digging. For example, if they say it's hard to get the classes you want or that the professors are distant, those are alarm bells. On the other hand, if they want you to know that they've found the way, the truth, and the life, that's great, but make sure that it is also for you. At St. John's College, where there are Great Books and no electives, I asked a couple of girls who'd transferred from the University of California at Berkeley if it bothered them that they couldn't have a course in psychology under someone like Eric Erikson at Harvard. The comeback was, "Oh no. We can go to the library and read all that." But the regimen that has been described as four years discussing what is truth is not for everybody.

• Are most classes lectures, with everyone madly taking notes to regurgitate on the next exam, or are they discussion? A great deal more work is required of both teacher and student in a discussion class. The teacher must have questions to cover every point he would make in a lecture. As a professor acquaintance said at a 2 A.M. breakup of a poker game, "Well, I'm not prepared; I'll have to lecture today." The student has to be prepared because he's expected to be a participant in the discussion class, not a passive ear.

• Do the students take an active part in the discussion or is the class lifeless? Don't depend on your observation of one or two classes for the answer to this; ask several students.

• Do the professors give essay or multiple-choice exams? The latter are easy-to-grade cop-outs. Many a state university student doesn't write a paper of any kind in four years. And that is inexcusable.

• After class, do any students hang around to ask questions or continue the discussion, or does everyone clear out pronto?

• Is there any discussion about what went on in class?

• Do they stay around after meals arguing? Or is the conversation about the weekend?

• What are the principal reasons students leave or transfer out? This is well worth asking even if the registrar or friends may not have gotten any reason for leaving, much less the right one. A common one is the desire for a major that the college doesn't offer, since students often change their interests. Often it's the desire to be in or near a city, or to be in a larger place. There is so much movement among institutions that one reason has to be that freshmen and sophomores often think the grass is greener on the other side of the fence. Freshmen may also say something akin to, "Half the freshman class is transferring out." Go to the registrar and ask how many requests he's had for transcripts to be sent to other institutions; maybe it'll be three or four. If dissatisfaction with the quality of the school comes to be the major reason, more specific inquiries will give you an indication whether you'd be unhappy too.

• What is the attrition rate? Some state institutions have lost as many as 80 percent of their freshmen in four years; in others 30 percent or more of the students don't return for the sophomore year. The popular University of Colorado graduates only 40 percent in four years. At the other end of the scale, some colleges graduate 80 or 90 percent of an entering class, and in between, a lot of good colleges lose 40 percent or more over four years. It is worthwhile finding out why students leave; it may be because they don't have the commitment to learning expected in that community; they want more bodies around; or, it may not be a very good place. You will have to decide whether the reasons are relevant to you.

• What kind of rapport is there between students and faculty? This is a key question. The ideal learning situation is one in which the student is heavily involved, not just a receptive ear. If there is the kind of close collaboration—and stimulus—that makes this possible, that fact will come out loud and clear. The students will refer to faculty members as valued mentors, bull-session participants, or advisers. If you see faculty members having coffee with students or meandering across campus with them, these are good signs.

• Ask a dozen or more students: If you came back here after graduation would you have good enough faculty friends that you might have dinner or spend a night at one of their homes? In a good undergraduate college most of the answers will be yes or there's something wrong. In a large school that question is more likely to provoke laughter, although at Washington University in St. Louis I asked twenty-two students that question and got twenty affirmative answers.

• Who does the teaching? If graduate assistants teach the required general education courses, the freshmen and sophomores are being cheated. If they're taught by senior faculty but in auditorium-size classes, that's better, but it's still short-changing the students because it's only a lecture. Graduate students are, with mighty few exceptions, untrained unsupervised mercenaries working on their own advanced degrees. Their primary interest is in their own degree, not yours, and they constitute a way of saving money at the expense of the undergraduate.

• How many part-time teachers are there?

• Are there any foreign teachers whose English is so poor

they are hard to understand? A Federal survey found that 41 percent of all faculty members are part-time, many of them aliens, unfamiliar with our culture or language. If there are a lot of part-time faculty, that is a black mark, for the temporary teacher has little or no loyalty or commitment to the school. He may be hard to find after class, and as an academic adviser worse than useless, because as one student told a member of Dr. Boyer's team visiting colleges, "They don't know how the college works."

• Is there any TV or programmed instruction where no instructor meets the class?

• What are class sizes, really? The institution may advertise a low student-faculty ratio, but don't buy that. Ask particularly about the courses that all or most freshmen or sophomores have to take.

• Are there any classes of one hundred; if so, how many? The answers will reveal pretty starkly an important difference between the college and the large university.

• Do faculty make themselves available after class and keep regular office hours or do they vanish? At Cornell University, for example, faculty members commonly take refuge in the graduate library, where undergraduates are not permitted. At many urban institutions they hurry home to the suburbs. In a small college town or on the campus of a small college there is no place for either student or teacher to hide.

• Does the faculty advising system really work? This is where practically every college fails at least some of the time.

• Do the advisers really advise, with a knowledge of the student's background and interests, or do they just initial class schedules? The answers will tell something about student-faculty relationships, which are crucial. Advising doesn't necessarily mean job counseling; that is the placement office's function. Undergraduates need help in understanding that their education is preparing them for a lifetime of work—and fulfillment—not just for a first job. A rapidly changing world has made mature advice on why they're there, what they are getting for princely tuitions, and how those courses will fit them for the world of work matters of far greater moment than they were forty or fifty years ago. And if students don't get some such advice they'll rightly think they've been gypped.

Two of the requisites of a good college experience are two continuing conversations. One is with your teachers, who ought to be mature individuals, competent in their fields, having a broad view of the world and an interest in the student. The second conversation, with one's peers, is a part of the process of internal exploration that college should be. The two together help in shaping values, attitudes, and aspirations, and are as crucial as the standards and the expectations of the classroom. The course content is something that evaporates over time.

• What is the learning atmosphere? Is learning the concern, or are grades? Is there intense competition for grades?

• Is cheating common, or is there an ethos or an honor code that condemns it?

• Is this a demanding or an easy place? A college may be easy or difficult to get into, but the central consideration is rigor. One may be a lot tougher to get into than to stay in, while another that's easy to get into may be more demanding. If it's easy, it's a sham. And it's a simple matter to find out by asking a few students how many hours a week they study, how many pages they read a night, and what the level of expectation is.

• Is it possible to study in your dorm rooms? Noisy dorms are not just an inconvenience; they are cause to shun the place. If there are no quiet hours it means learning is not very important here. Fun and games come first.

• What percentage of students leave campus on weekends? If it's a suitcase college, the parking lots become deserted Thursday afternoon or Friday and the sense of community is diluted or nonexistent. If most everybody clears out every weekend, it also says something about the amount of work expected of them.

• What is the social life like? Are there dominant social groups, such as fraternities, and if so is it easy to move among them, or are they tightly cloistered? Is it possible to be editor of the paper or class president and not be a member?

• Are athletics only for the hired jocks, or do a substantial number of the paying students have the fun of playing on varsity and intramural teams? In other words, is the big football weekend the only athletic event the student body takes an interest in?

• Is there a variety of campus activities and imported speakers, music, and other cultural events? In most good colleges, the answers to that question are affirmative; in fact, many campuses offer more such variety than the nearby town or city.

• Do the students take advantage of these activities? This often destroys the frequent complaint that "there's nothing to do here." And of course it says something about the students.

• What is the drinking, the drug, and the sex scene? Would a person of your beliefs be comfortable here?

• Does the place favor anonymity and conformity or does it encourage identity and individualism? Does it coddle or challenge? Colleges will differ startlingly. For example, Antioch is a place that values tolerance for diversity, democratic governance, and concern for improving society, but West Point does not. Antioch wouldn't take any prizes for esprit, such as feelings of well-being for or loyalty to the institution, while West Point would.

Teenagers often say they don't want to be a number in a big school, or just as often they say they don't want a college smaller than their suburban high school. The fear of being a number may mask apprehensions about competing with a dauntingly large number of very able peers, while wanting a college larger than your high school may reveal fear of the close scrutiny you might get as a person in a college with high expectations where everyone is clearly visible and weighed. But just about every Grade A undergraduate college is smaller than the suburban high school.

The visitor should come to terms with himself on this score because a principal benefit of a good college is finding out who one is, what he or she wants to become, and maybe taking a step or two on the road toward becoming that kind of person. As the catalog of the exciting but late lamented Kirkland College—now absorbed by Hamilton—once said, "College is a time of internal exploration and the small, familial community is more conducive to that."

• Does the school have good faculty people across the board, not just in the major you want?

• Are the special opportunities, like off-campus programs, doing research with a faculty member, or independent study, readily available, or are they just on paper?

Wanting a major the college doesn't offer is frequently a cause of transferring, and often as not it is not a good reason. For one thing, most students change majors at least once. For another, only about one person in ten is doing anything at age fifty that he was interested in as a freshman. And again, he should be getting a good broad education now; the specialization should come later.

• How easy is it to get the classes you want at registration? Or is it even possible? It isn't possible at many big institutions.

Questions to Ask Faculty and Administrators

• What happens to the graduates? What percentages go on to graduate and professional schools? What percentage goes into business or teaching?

• Does the college have a good career counseling office and placement director that works closely with students *throughout* their college days, not just at the end? The career counseling office should complement and supplement the faculty adviser. Does his office have a good pipeline to the job market?

• What has been the graduates' record in getting jobs, what kinds, where, and at what salary levels?

• What is the record in graduate and professional school acceptances?

- Does the college take a healthy pride in itself, or is it so smugly sure of itself as to be chauvinistic?
- Does it have a "reject morale" because it was a fallback or a safety school for a number of the students?
- Ask the librarian about the extent of library usage. It may be nearly empty during the middle of the day and crowded early in the morning or at night. Are more students playing the pinball or the video game machines in the student center than are using the library?
- Ask faculty members what they think of the students, how they compare them with students at other places they've taught. And ask them what percentages of the ones they teach are interested in learning.

College should be a place of diverse people and views and beliefs. It should be a place where faculty take an interest in campus programs outside of the classroom. It should be a place of debate, questioning, and discussion. It should have some feeling of family or community.

And when you visit you are the customer. Any question that is important to you deserves a full and candid answer. If, with a reasonable effort, you don't get it, that's a black mark against the school, but the chances are you'll get more than you expected.

8

Some Proof
of the Pudding

The Performance Records of a
Lot of Davids Outdo the Goliaths.

What proof is there that some little-known colleges might be better investments than famous and popular ones?

Assuming that the purpose of college is to educate, the good college is the one that has an effect on the student. It should be judged by the kind of people it turns out rather than by the kind it takes in. But colleges aren't held to any such account-ability. Although then Education Secretary William Bennett raised academic hackles with such demands, his has by no means been the only voice saying colleges have a responsibility to show what they've accomplished. There is evidence aplenty on the fraction of applicants colleges accept and their high school grades and SAT scores, but not a word on what kind of human beings they are, and very limited information, but much myth, on what they achieve or contribute later on as adults.

The world of higher education is a status-conscious one, full of claims to achievement and excellence, but precious few colleges are able to give an Iacocca–style seventy-thousand-mile guarantee. And that's because they haven't done what ought to be their required homework: getting performance data on their products. Without such it is pretty difficult to assess the kind of effect the college experience has had on a youth and that is one big reason why myths hold such sway. Because it would be such a help to me, I have from time to time tried in vain to bug college presidents into spending some nuts-and-bolts research money to find out what has happened to their graduates.

But until much more of that is done, there are some tangibles that indicate the kind of people a college turns out. And that, over the long pull, is more important to the buyer than how outstanding are the seniors it accepts from high school. These indicators are the easily quantified ones where counts are kept: things like acceptance rates at graduate and professional schools, percentages going on to get doctorates, and winners of major graduate awards. The credentials of the doer only become visible later when his play is produced or he becomes chief executive officer or his contribution to society is recognized. And unless the colleges make an effort to ask, there'll be no count of how many graduates lead fuller, more satisfying lives as a result of their college experience.

A significant tangible is that of future Ph.D.'s. For instance, when a college barely thirty years old and not very selective for most of that time graduates a higher percentage who go on to win that achievement than all but a couple of score of other colleges—as Eckerd College has done—something out of the ordinary is happening; it clearly is having an effect on the youths who go there because it hasn't had the luxury that more famous colleges do of handpicking the ready-made achievers.

If Eckerd is producing so many future scholars and scientists, it must be revving up the intellectual metabolism of all of its students, raising both their aspirations and abilities. After all, everybody is living in the same academic family, influenced by the same ethos and standards, whether headed for the intellectual life or not. In fact, on a visit there a few years ago, a girl approached me to ask, "Do you know of a school I can go to where most of the class isn't majoring in business and economics?" At a time when those were fast becoming the most popular majors nationwide, just 15 percent of Eckerd's graduates went to business schools. But to her the temple was full of money changers. I told her, "Antioch, Reed, New, and St. John's would be about the only safe bets I can think of offhand, and maybe Berea, Oberlin, Swarthmore, and some you've never heard of: Berry, Deep Springs, Goddard, Marlboro, St. Olaf, and Thomas Aquinas."

Medical school acceptances offer one solid evidence that there's little magic in a name. Although veterinary school and doctoral programs in clinical psychology have been more selective and artificial intelligence now is, medical school was long the most popular professional choice. It used to seem that every third youth I talked to coveted the wealth and status of the physician. So when the medical schools were at their peak of selectivity, I sought some measure of assurance for my clients that the name of the college wasn't the factor that was going to determine their fate.

A friend running the American Medical Colleges Association applicant pool—which handled over 80 percent of all applications—did a check to see if he could find any instance where a Harvard applicant was favored simply because he was Harvard. He found that one medical school had arbitrarily given a Harvard senior credit for a B average (3.0) in his science courses when he actually had a 2.9 in them but an overall 3.0 average.

Having evidence that the name of the school wasn't the key, I managed to get a tabulation of the Medical College Aptitude Test scores for every institution in the country for eight consecutive tests to see which colleges had the most successful test-takers. A score of at least 550 on the science part was usually needed for acceptance. And on the theory that the science score reflected the college's input, whereas the verbal and mathematical scores pretty much reflected the high school Scholastic Aptitude Test, I compiled a list of all colleges whose seniors had averaged 550 or better on the science part. Of sixty-six on the list, forty-four were undergraduate colleges, and eleven of those had been selective only at the crest of the college-going boom. The list I compiled from those test scores appears in Table A (page 115).

Many prestige and "hot" colleges didn't get on the scoreboard. Some that didn't were Emory, Georgetown, Michigan, Rutgers, Tulane, Vanderbilt, Vermont, Virginia, and Wisconsin. Northwestern was the only one in the Big Ten to make it, Penn State and Delaware the only state institutions outside of California.

Some very selective colleges also didn't make it: Bates, Colby, Bucknell, Davidson, Dickinson, Furman, Miami University, Vassar, Wake Forest, William and Mary, and Washington and Lee. But it should also be noted that a lot of good colleges not on the list have medical school acceptance rates of 80 percent or better against a national average of 33 percent.

So, if some colleges that admit 80 to 90 percent of their applicants do at least as good a job in this stiff competition as the choosiest ones, that should comfort the college seeker who's not a top student. It argues that something good is taking place in the classrooms and on the campuses of many less selective colleges. Faculty members must be making some contribution to their students' growth. It also says that Wabash and Western Maryland, for example—so far as this measure is concerned—don't have to take a back seat to Princeton, Stanford, and a lot of others.

Some not very selective colleges that weren't on the list nevertheless had perfect or near-perfect medical school acceptance rates: Antioch for one had a 100 percent success rate two years in a row, while at Earlham, Knox, and Wooster, among others, nearly 90 percent of all who applied were accepted. Why did these Davids fare so well? Because they were and are held in high regard in the academic world, which knows quality when it sees it.

Possibly of less immediate interest to aspiring doctors, but

TABLE A

The sixty-six colleges whose medical school applicants' scores on the science part of the Medical Test averaged 550 or over for eight administrations of the test.

CalTech	628	Lafayette	568
Brooklyn College	616	Columbia	567
Harvey Mudd	615	Franklin and Marshall	567
Yeshiva	613	Johns Hopkins	566
Chicago	608	Radcliffe	566
Cornell U.	600	Muhlenberg	565
		Haverford	563
Queens	596	Dartmouth	562
Rennselaer	596	McMurry (Texas)	562
MIT	596	Williams	562
Cooper Union	592	Duke	561
Yale	590	Wesleyan	560
Brown	588	Bowdoin	560
Pembroke	586	Middlebury	560
Carleton	585	Colgate	560
Rice	585	Trinity (Conn.)	560
Swarthmore	584	Penn	560
Pomona	583		
Harvard	582	Grinnell	559
Augsburg	581	Ohio Wesleyan	558
		Northwestern	558
Brandeis	579	UCLA	557
Clarkson	579	Berkeley	557
Wabash	578	Calvin	556
Union	577	St. Thomas (Minn.)	555
Barnard	576	Boston College	554
Hamilton	576	Illinois Institute	
Rochester	575	of Technology	553
Western Maryland	575	Wooster	553
Lehigh	572	UC-Davis	553
Oberlin	572	UC-SC	551
Occidental	572	Penn State	550
Reed	572	Delaware	550
Princeton	570	Washington U. (St. Louis)	550
Stanford	570	Denison	550

in an area of far greater national significance and concern, is that the good liberal arts colleges are outperforming even the top twenty research universities in turning out the high quality scientists that the country badly needs and whose supply has been shrinking. The situation has grown serious enough that two of its leaders have warned the scientific community that a lot of its most treasured big-ticket projects, such as a multi-billion-dollar super collider for high-energy physics research and a space station, among others, should be cut back or give way to science's most urgent need: producing more scientists. Dr. Frank Press, president of the National Academy of Sciences, and Dr. Robert M. Rosenzweig, president of the Association of American Universities, whose members include fifty-four major research universities, even advocated what to the scientific community is heresy: setting priorities. Scientists lobby eagerly for their own projects but adamantly refuse to have them ranked against others. These leaders said that important as these projects are, there is more to do than the country is willing to pay for and choices will have to be made. For the nation's good, both said, educating more scientists should be number one on the list.

The United States has been losing ground to foreign countries in the global race to turn new scientific knowledge into new military and industrial technologies and commercial products. And the pace is quickening. For example, more new mathematics has been created in the last few decades than in the previous two centuries. New math concepts made space travel possible by reason of the doors it opened in physics. It is no wonder knowledge is exploding: 97 percent of all the mathematicians who've ever lived are alive today. So breakthroughs in scientific knowledge are coming faster than ever in history; moreover, the time gap between a scientific discovery and its practical application in the form of a light bulb or a computer has shrunk from several decades to a few years.

Not only is the number of future scientists in the colleges and universities shrinking, but also a large proportion of them are foreign students who will return to their own countries and make them tougher competitors. In some Southwestern and Western institutions, for example, as many as 80 percent of the engineering students are foreign, mostly from Asian countries, and they also account for a large part of the mathematicians.

Both the public and the legislators, who should be better informed, have always perceived the top research universities as the nation's seedbeds of scholars and scientists. But they are not. Ever since 1920, all the data that researchers have dug up have showed that the good liberal arts colleges are the richest sources. Some of the universities' own faculty have been saying so for a long time, but few outside the colleges bothered to listen or to believe it.

In the sixty-odd years since the National Academy of Sciences started keeping tabs on the sources of American scientists and scholars, the undergraduate colleges have markedly outperformed the universities in the percentages and sometimes even in the total numbers of graduates going on to get doctorates in all fields, not just in the sciences. Twenty years ago, a Congressional committee report pushing for a larger share of funds for the productive schools said there was "absolutely no relationship between the allocation of Federal science education funds and improvement in the quality of undergraduate teaching." It said that the popular assumption was that the universities were the prime source, but that in reality the reverse was true. Using prizes and awards won for graduate study as criteria, the committee found that thirty-four of the top fifty institutions were colleges. And of the sixteen universities, five were technical institutions specializing in the sciences.

Finally, in 1985, a group of undergraduate colleges, pushed into it by severe money worries, made a concerted effort to tell their story. In this company, chest-beating isn't genteel. Colleges use every tool of marketing to compete for the supply of teenagers, but their code makes it unprofessional and gauche to tell the world how good they are or how the competition falls short. So they make no invidious comparisons with the assembly-line universities, either in quality of undergraduate experience or in productivity of useful citizens. A college president is loath to declare publicly that a student is lucky to get the time of day from a university faculty member, or that a place like Earlham, Eckerd, Wooster, Hampshire, or Guilford make the big ones look like inferior merchandise.

The presidents of forty-eight colleges met at Oberlin in 1985 to call attention to the clear superiority of their institutions for the education of scientists and to press their case for a fairer share of Federal help. After a long period of Reagan cutbacks, the colleges' science facilities faced the need for billion-dollar infusions of money to maintain their standards. The colleges, unlike the universities, pretty much pay their own way. Only 15 percent of their cost of laboratory equipment comes from Washington, whereas the twenty top research universities get 52 percent. Because of their big staffs and extensive laboratories and because they have the clout, the universities win the lush research grants that pay them so handsomely.

It took Oberlin provost Sam C. Carrier, and David Davis-Van Atta, its director of institutional research, two years to dig up the facts for their story because so little had been done to discover the outcomes of the college experience. That is one reason why so many good schools have so long been underestimated. The Carrier and Davis-Van Atta figures were updated in 1987.

What they documented was that fifty small colleges outdo twenty top-rated research universities—most of them big—in producing scientists. And when quality is compared, the colleges rank at or near the top of all institutions. Of the top ten in quality of product, six are colleges. The fifty colleges are listed in Table B (page 119).

It isn't surprising that the universities get the credit for being the greenhouses for scientists when the academicians themselves don't know the story. As Mr. Carrier said, "I always knew that these colleges were productive in that area, but the magnitude of their productivity surprised me."

TABLE B

The fifty liberal arts colleges participating in the Oberlin
conference on the future of science at liberal arts colleges.

Albion	Kalamazoo
Alma	Kenyon
Amherst	Lafayette
Antioch	Macalester
Barnard	Manhattan
Bates	Middlebury
Beloit	Mount Holyoke
Bowdoin	Oberlin
Bryn Mawr	Occidental
Bucknell	Ohio Wesleyan
Carleton	Pomona
Colgate	Reed
Colorado	Smith
Davidson	St. Olaf
Denison	Swarthmore
DePauw	Trinity (Conn.)
Earlham	Union
Franklin and Marshall	Vassar
Grinnell	Wabash
Hamilton	Wellesley
Hampton University	Wesleyan
Harvey Mudd	Wheaton (Ill.)
Haverford	Whitman
Holy Cross	Williams
Hope	Wooster

Although interest in the sciences has been declining nationally since the mid-seventies, the colleges' production of science
degrees rose 16 percent, but in the research universities it
dropped 14 percent. Furthermore, in the colleges, 15.2 percent
of the women became science majors; in the universities 11
percent.

A full 25 percent of all recent graduates of the colleges were
science majors, half again that of the twenty universities. "A

most significant point," the 1987 report said, "is the approximate equivalency between the 50 liberal arts colleges and the 20 top-rated universities in absolute volume. . . ."

What's more, the Oberlin report said, the quality of the liberal arts scientists has been as good as those of the universities. It used six criteria, such as National Science Foundation fellowships, listings in the directories of leading scientists, and membership in the prestigious National Academy of Sciences, to show that these colleges "unfailingly ranked equally with the best universities at the undergraduate level." Indeed, most of the top twenty-five institutions turned out to be colleges. When all fifty colleges were compared with all twenty universities, the latter held an edge so modest as not to permit any bragging rights. In short, the report said, the colleges are "clearly" producing scientists as good as those from the best research universities.

In an article on the origins of American scientists, the *Accounts of Chemical Research* said, "The data in these reports demonstrate that . . . those [institutions] that are excellent for graduate education turn out to be less excellent for undergraduate education."

The top universities didn't even produce many of their own faculty. Only 18 percent were undergraduates of one of the top twenty. But 30 percent of them had gone to one of the fifty colleges. Furthermore, professors from Harvard and the universities of California and Texas who took part in the Oberlin study made a point of saying that the quality of education in the good small liberal arts colleges such as they had attended was "unparalleled during this crucial development period."

In his introduction to the report, Oberlin president Frederick Starr made a point that everyone looking at colleges, whatever his field of interest, should keep in mind. The success of these colleges, he wrote, "is due significantly to the close link between teaching and faculty research that exists on such campuses. No amount of research and scholarly activity will benefit the undergraduate if this vital interaction does not take place in significant quantity. Such contact with distinguished faculty is perhaps the primary hallmark of undergraduate science education at the 48 liberal arts colleges."

The conditions conducive to highest quality science education, as Dr. Boyer's team had said in their book, *College*, "are typically not found at major research universities." College faculty devote nearly 55 percent of their time to teaching. At the universities faculty spend 33 percent of their time in research and only 29.6 percent teaching, which includes substantial teaching of graduate students.

The Oberlin study demonstrated that student participation in research is far, far greater at the colleges. It found that nearly one third of the nearly seven thousand professional journal articles by faculty in the forty-eight colleges over a five-year period had been co-authored by students. Students also co-authored 8 of the 351 books published by faculty members and one in five of the papers presented to professional meetings.

While comparable data for the universities are sparse, an article in *Chemical and Engineering News* quoted Robert West, professor of chemistry at the University of Wisconsin, as noting that less than 1 percent of the undergraduates carry out research in chemistry in any one year, and that only "about four to five percent of the chemistry papers published by UW scientists had been co-authored by undergraduates." West said that "a major disadvantage is that undergraduates require a lot of supervision and training; the return on the time and money invested in them is seen as not worthwhile."

In 1987 the University of Colorado's undergraduate research program had forty-six students in thirty-five departments involved in a school of over twenty thousand students. Applicants literally have to go through the process of applying for and winning a grant, whereas in the good small college almost any serious student with the desire can get involved in research with a faculty member.

The Colorado program is patterned after programs at MIT, UCLA, Stanford, and the University of Minnesota.

While the Oberlin findings applied only to the science area, a much broader study about the same time demonstrated that schools that have high standards in one area are likely to have them across the board. The twelve colleges of the Great Lakes Colleges Association commissioned Carol H. Fuller to find out which of fifteen hundred colleges and universities had produced the highest percentages of graduates who went on to earn Ph.D.'s in all fields between 1951 and 1980. Not only were most of them liberal arts colleges, but many were colleges that have never been particularly selective. The ranking of the top fifty appears in Table C (page 123).

Three leading technical institutions headed the list because of their heavy productivity in the sciences, but they weren't in the competition in the humanities.

Dr. Fuller also discovered that the colleges in the Great Lakes association were far more productive of scholars and scientists than the eight Ivy League universities. And the twelve colleges of the Associated Colleges of the Midwest outdid the leading universities of their region, the Big Ten.

Having shown that "little David was small, but oh my!", Dr. Fuller urged some broader consumer research that is long overdue; namely, finding out which colleges or universities have turned out the leading corporate executives, political leaders, winners of various prizes and recognitions, and people with a special commitment to service, such as Peace Corps volunteers.

The nearest approximation of such data that is readily available are the listings in *Who's Who*, a compendium of high-ranking national and state government and judicial officers, top-ranking military officers, high-ranking officials of major cities, and the elite of business, cultural, church, educational, philanthropic, and professional organizations, as well as recipients of major honorary awards and such prizes as the Nobel and Pulitzer. It is not possible to get a mention by buying the directory.

A search of the eighty thousand listings in the 1988–1989 edition, completed for this book, make the small colleges—

TABLE C

Top fifty institutions in Ph.D. productivity, 1951–1980, based on percentage of graduates.

	ALL FIELDS		HUMANITIES		SCIENCE	
	Total	Percent of Graduates	Total	Percent of Graduates	Total	Percent of Graduates
Harvey Mudd	257	40.7	5	0.8	247	39.1
Caltech	1818	40.0	17	0.4	1781	39.2
Reed	968	25.3	154	4.0	766	20.0
MIT	5438	20.9	114	0.4	5141	19.8
Swarthmore	1418	20.9	350	5.2	975	14.4
Haverford	683	18.8	196	5.4	415	11.4
Oberlin	2321	17.8	666	5.1	1347	10.3
New College (Fla.)	63	16.1	13	3.3	48	12.2
Chicago	3805	15.6	781	3.2	2592	10.6
UC–San Diego	362	14.1	28	1.1	325	12.6
Amherst	1118	13.7	363	4.5	642	7.9
Carleton	993	13.7	253	3.5	631	8.7
Cooper Union	602	13.7	3	0.1	586	13.4
Pomona	1066	13.7	224	2.9	713	9.2
Brandeis	893	13.5	218	3.3	578	8.7
Wabash (Ind.)	501	12.9	105	2.7	324	8.4
Rice	1501	12.4	229	1.9	1192	9.9
Webb Institute (N.Y.)	52	12.4	1	0.2	47	11.2
Wesleyan (Conn.)	877	12.4	255	3.6	511	7.2
Bryn Mawr	593	12.0	282	5.7	276	5.6
Princeton	2713	11.7	741	3.2	1765	7.6
Grinnell	706	11.4	168	2.7	450	7.3
UC–Irvine	299	11.3	37	1.4	253	9.5
Eckerd	119	11.2	33	3.1	77	7.2
Antioch	875	11.0	131	1.7	620	7.8
UC–Riverside	897	11.0	126	1.5	709	8.7
St. John's (Md.)	117	10.4	55	4.9	49	4.4
Wooster	868	10.4	190	2.3	517	6.2
Radcliffe	923	10.2	357	3.9	469	5.2
Davidson	599	9.9	179	2.9	306	5.0
Williams	835	9.8	255	3.0	507	6.0

TABLE C (cont.)

Top fifty institutions in Ph.D. productivity, 1951–1980, based on percentage of graduates.

| | ALL FIELDS | | HUMANITIES | | SCIENCE | |
	Total	Percent of Graduates	Total	Percent of Graduates	Total	Percent of Graduates
New School (N.Y.)	99	9.7	30	2.9	57	5.6
Barnard	1163	9.5	426	3.5	590	4.8
Hamilton (N.Y.)	507	9.4	181	3.3	255	4.7
Kalamazoo (Mich.)	427	9.3	70	1.5	307	6.7
Earlham	476	9.1	87	1.7	308	5.9
Harvard	5554	9.0	1551	2.5	3527	5.7
Rensselaer Polytechnic Institute	1929	9.0	26	0.1	1819	8.5
Bowdoin	578	8.8	156	2.4	345	5.3
UC–Santa Cruz	262	8.8	59	2.0	192	6.5
Cornell	5329	8.8	595	1.0	4213	7.0
Johns Hopkins	1524	8.7	204	1.2	1207	6.9
CUNY: City College	6893	8.6	797	1.0	4990	6.2
Rochester	2056	8.4	483	2.0	1288	5.3
Wellesley	1002	8.4	390	3.3	461	3.9
Yale	3407	8.4	1085	2.7	1996	4.9
Brown	1977	8.3	405	1.7	1388	5.8
Carnegie-Mellon	1678	8.3	90	0.4	1422	7.0
Occidental	780	8.2	134	1.4	464	4.9
Kenyon	348	7.9	120	2.7	202	4.6
Group Total	70269	11.0	13418	2.0	49890	7.9

and often the little-known ones—look as dramatically superior to the universities in the world of doers as in the world of savants and scientists. Of course, *Who's Who* listings are just one more indication, but they do buttress and complement the small-college claims that they are the stone the builders rejected that has become the head of the corner.

This, however, is not news; in general our findings restate those of a search made thirty years ago by the Educational Records Bureau (ERB) in New York. With Easterners panicking about getting into a good college, the ERB did a search of the 1956–1967 *Who's Who* "to discover whether there were good colleges outside of the East." The answer was an emphatic yes, based on the production of achieving alumni.

That survey, like this one, found that Yale led the list, with Harvard and Princeton close behind. Amherst, Oberlin, and Williams were virtually tied for fourth. Of the top sixty colleges, forty-nine were in the West, Midwest, and South, and most of them were colleges with names unfamiliar to people in other parts of the country.

For this survey, the average number of graduates for 1980–1986 was multiplied by twenty, to get a workable base number, and then divided by the number of *Who's Who* mentions. This produced fifty-nine schools with index numbers below one hundred. Only eighteen of them were universities, and twenty-nine were in the West, Midwest, and South. This does not do justice to several colleges that in recent years have changed character by going coed, like Vassar or Sarah Lawrence, or that are still too young, like Hampshire, Pitzer, or Eckerd, to have a sizable body of mature alumni.

Here is the list, with the index number for each:

13	Yale	41	Oberlin
15	Harvard	44	Reed
16	Princeton		Stanford
20	Chicago	49	Davidson
21	Caltech	50	DePauw
23	Amherst	52	Wesleyan
24	Williams	53	Northwestern
25	Columbia		Pomona
27	CCNY	55	Cooper Union
	Swarthmore	56	Wabash
29	Dartmouth	57	Wheaton (Ill.)
30	MIT	58	St. John's College
36	Haverford		Holy Cross
	Washington and Lee	59	Johns Hopkins

61	Hamilton
	NYU
66	Colgate
67	Antioch
68	Pennsylvania (U. of)
69	Bowdoin
71	Brown
72	Knox
74	Ohio Wesleyan
76	Carleton
77	Union
	Virginia Military Institute
	Grinnell
	Vanderbilt
78	Hampden-Sydney
	Bryn Mawr

80	Cornell College (Iowa)
84	Kenyon
	Sewanee (U. of the South)
86	Beloit
87	Duke
88	Wooster
89	Washington U. (St. Louis)
92	Illinois Institute of Technology
93	Occidental
95	Notre Dame
	Rice
	Millsaps
97	Denison
	Franklin and Marshall
98	Bard

The best-known universities with index numbers under two hundred were:

104	Michigan
105	Georgetown
109	Fordham
112	Catholic
125	Carnegie-Mellon
126	Wisconsin
128	Syracuse
133	George Washington
134	Rochester
137	Tulane

138	Illinois
139	UC–Berkeley
140	Emory
146	North Carolina
150	Southern Methodist
156	Minnesota
158	Tufts
163	Virginia
174	Case Western

Quite a few of the very popular universities did poorly:

202	Texas
205	Georgia Tech
208	Southern California
	William and Mary
233	Miami (Ohio)
251	Rensselaer

256	U. of Washington
260	Ohio State
267	Indiana
268	Colorado
277	Boston College
280	Boston U.

And some well-known universities ought to be ashamed:

313	Miami (Florida)	463	Kentucky
349	Connecticut	474	Georgia
361	Rutgers	489	Vermont
393	Drexel	629	Maryland
395	Penn State	694	American
397	Michigan State	1011	New Hampshire
400	Florida	1065	Delaware
426	Texas A & M		

Furthermore, some of the top-ranked research universities hardly got on the scoreboard.

The small colleges do far better for the student than the state universities in the quality of life outside of class too. Donald O'Dowd, president of the University of Alaska, when he was executive vice chancellor of the vast State University of New York system, was quoted in *The New York Times* as saying:

"In exchange for higher cost, students at private institutions usually get a richer array of services, including better student-teacher ratios, better student life and athletic programs than are possible with the funds available at public institutions."

George Drake, president of Grinnell College, writing in *The Chronicle of Higher Education*, pointed out that most small colleges offer more varsity sports for more students than do state universities. This may come as a surprise, but "fewer than five percent of the students at large universities participate in varsity sports, whereas at small colleges the figure is close to 40 percent." And when intramurals are included, the majority of students are involved.

In 1889, in the first football game west of the Mississippi, Grinnell beat the University of Iowa 24–0 in a game played by students "and maybe a ringer or two for the fun of it." But since then, Drake added, "a chasm has opened. . . . Big-time inter-collegiate sports have become the property of the public. They are entertainment for the millions rather than extracurricular outlets for students." In small colleges all varsity sports are supported from general funds because athletics are part of the educational program, "and athletics are educational. . . . The contrast could not be starker."

In their nationally televised football game commercials, the major university's blurb may show students walking across a well-treed campus with the narrator saying something like, for example, "Michigan State's excellent academics are complemented by athletics." Malarkey. Students at Michigan State are even less involved in intercollegiate athletics than they are in their own educations, unless they're in one of the elite residential colleges.

Martha Peterson, who had been a dean at the University of Wisconsin before becoming president of Barnard and later of Beloit, became a convert to the small colleges, which she says "are special places of teaching and learning . . . in which the teacher and learner face each other almost daily. Formally or informally, they pursue knowledge, explore ideas, ask questions, explore current events, and share personal experiences. There is no place on the small college campus for either the professor or the student to hide. The years spent in such a challenging, non-anonymous environment offer unparalleled preparation for living in an unpredictable world."

A search could reveal millions of cases like that of a client father who said, "I went to Marquette; the doctor next to me graduated with honors from Yale. We're both doing the same work." In short, the clout is not in the name, the size, or the place of the college; it is in the student himself, and the best college is the one that will contribute most effectively to his growth and development in these last and crucial formative years of youth.

9 ✍

The Ground Rules
Have Changed on
What College Can Do

What Counts Is the
Experience, Not the Label.

For several decades, ours has been an establishment economy, governed by its rules, and comfortable and predictable for those who belonged, so the object has been to get "in" by way of the proper schools, the proper courses, and the proper contacts. That system is now in the process of being overwhelmed by a frontier economy. New knowledge, not land or capital or machines, is the new frontier, and the successful pioneers are those with the brains prepared to exploit it.

The government agencies that keep track of such matters have already pointed out that industry, or making things, is now only a third as large or important as services, or providing things. Services means professionals of all kinds working in a knowledge society. And it operates on competence, rather than contacts.

The startling fact is that most of the jobs in today's economy, like most of the drugs on the pharmacist's shelves, weren't there before World War II. And in a very short time—by the turn of the century—most college graduates will be working at jobs that don't exist now while they are in college. Even AT&T, that Blue Chip Establishment bastion, which made its reputation on being dependably the same and on making phones that had to last, and where employees on Monday "were sure what Tuesday would bring," works in a different world now. Within eighteen months after the court-ordered breakup, its entire product line had changed, and the end is nowhere in sight.

In 1981, the noted sociologist Peter Drucker wrote: "For thirty years, employers have been hiring graduates for their degrees rather than their capabilities. Employment, pay, and even promotion have depended on one's diploma." But in the 1990s, he predicted, "the battle cry . . . will be the demand for performance and accountability."

Drucker's prediction was too conservative; the demand is already in full cry. Many major employers have interviewing regimens that test the applicant's ability to write, speak, and think, as well as his knowledge. Indeed, the interviewing process is often the most important part of the hiring decision; more important than the major, the grade point average, or the name of the college.

In this kind of evaluation, the labels on the courses or the names of the schools become less relevant; what counts is what the college has done to develop the powers of the applicant. However, getting hired for the first job is only the first page of the story. There will be other jobs with greater demands. And less than five years out of school it is a person's own abilities that are decisive.

Just as territorial expansion and industrialization were the forces of eighteenth- and nineteenth-century growth, so new knowledge is the power behind present and future growth. Already, nine out of ten people change jobs two to four or more times in a career, and often into fields that are brand new. By leaps and bounds, power and wealth have been springing from these new ventures. The rate of change, moreover, will only quicken because there's so much more brainpower at work than ever before. Mathematics is the basic tool that makes possible advances in other sciences: space travel and the supercomputer, for example. And as in mathematics, about 97 percent of all the scientists who have ever lived are working today.

Neuroscientists have created "creatures" with eyes, brains, and arms, and with senses of touch and vision that can move on their own and are free to behave in their own world. As Dr. Gerald M. Edelman, one of the creators, said, "We have learned more about the brain in the last ten years than in all history."

Equally important, scientific findings are soon translated into new technology and commercial applications. In *The New York Times,* science writer William J. Broad reported that experts believe we have reached a turning point in the history of invention because—unlike in the past—inventors are dramatically increasing their reliance on basic scientific research to compete in the global race for commercial innovations. In fact, scientific discoveries and the development of their practical applications are starting to merge.

In the past, technical breakthroughs such as the plow, the printing press, the steam engine, and the landmark inventions of the eighteenth and early nineteenth centuries were the work of ingenious tinkerers and enterprisers. Things began to change in the nineteenth century, but even so, fifty years elapsed between the discovery of the electric generator in 1830 and electric lights. The gap between Einstein's theory of relativity and the atomic bomb was forty years; between the discovery of the master molecule of life, DNA, and commercial genetic engineering, twenty years. But it was only six years between the 1957 discovery of the electron's abilities and the commercial production of electrical diodes for transistor radios and computers.

In short, scientific discovery and a resulting technology now almost go hand in glove. Some American patents, Mr. Broad continues, cite fifty or more scientific papers, twice as many as in Japan and far ahead of Britain, France, or Germany. And because America leads the world in basic research and development, the gap between a scientific paper and a commercial patent has shrunk in this country to about six years.

The Nobel Prize committee endorsed the idea that this is a different world when it gave the 1987 prize in economics to Dr. Robert Solow, who demonstrated that growth is not coming from increases in the quantity of capital or machines—the old gospel—but from the increase in knowledge and the resulting advances in technology and human skills and understanding.

This was a scholarly affirmation of the Bureau of Labor Statistics' nuts-and-bolts prediction that nine out of every ten jobs will soon be in the service industries, which is another way of categorizing the professional, the technical, and the managerial jobs that college graduates are and will be filling. The professionals will soon be outnumbering the blue-collar workers for the first time in history.

And opportunities for these professionals, says Samuel Ehrenhalt, a Bureau official, will depend more than ever on creativity, independent thought and action, and above all on their stock of knowledge and their ideas. This is a lot different than pinning one's hopes on connections or college prestige.

Change is also shifting power and wealth geographically, from the Establishment Northeast to the nouveau Southwest and elsewhere. A new kind of economy plus a shift to new areas creates new kinds of opportunities, bypassing or dislodging old arrangements and old-boy networks in favor of the prepared and the alert individual.

Just how great is the flux and how small are the chances of counting on a specific career in a specific job ten or twenty years from now is dramatically illustrated by the case history of an exceedingly select group, the Yale class of 1957. This was truly an elite group, chosen when the competition for admission was peaking. Only about one out of six top-notch applicants made it. These able men, at their twenty-fifth reunion in 1982, found that three quarters of them were working in jobs that hadn't even existed when they were in college. And if that was true for the class of 1957, it will be true in spades, doubled and redoubled, for the classes of 1997 and 2007.

In other words, change has already gone farther and faster than is generally realized. Wealth and power are shifting to the pioneers, the risk-takers, the innovators.

In a fascinating anatomy lesson on sixteen elite boarding schools, *Preparing for Power,* Peter W. Cookson, Jr., and Caroline Hodges Persell show that when youngsters, who tend to be children of rich and powerful parents, come out of these schools prepped for the elite colleges, they have gone on in disproportionate numbers to the boardrooms, the bar associations, and the bureaucracies that run the country. For a long time these schools largely served, and discriminated in favor of, Establishment scions, functioning as a kind of farm system or Little League for the Ivy League. There the children of the upper class met—and still meet—the right people and made the connections that would serve well later on, whether in New York or Washington.

But, the authors say, in the process of living a tightly regimented existence designed to fulfill the aims of the institution and the class for which these children are being prepared, they are stripped of individuality and sense of privacy. Instead they are instilled with a group identity that begins in the dormitories, the classrooms, and the playing fields, but doesn't end with graduation. It "continues to grow, becoming more interwoven, entangled, and in the end the basis of status group and class solidarity."

The authors say that "the structured, almost prison-like quality of boarding school socializes some students for lives as prisoners of their class. After prep school they will go to the right college, marry the right man or woman, get the right job, join the right clubs, travel to the right places, and grow weary in the right style. Thus the cycle of socialization recreates generations of individuals whose potentials are often crippled, not freed, by privilege."

However, some come out healthy, if disaffected. In general,

these exceptions have been the individualistic and creative graduates, and they hold few fond memories about the time they spent in prep school.

In the closing chapter, after reporting that the goal of the largest group of students was to become a business manager, the authors ask, "For what kind of a life is the prep rite of passage the best preparation? Does it develop successful entrepreneurs and risk-takers? Does it encourage innovative scientists or inventors?"

Then, after citing the stagnation of the British economy and suggesting a connection with the rigidity of England's class structure, they go on, "In a period of economic scarcity and stagnation we might expect the prep experience to become relatively more important, as those already holding power try to cling to what they have. Yet if we are entering an era of unprecedented growth and prosperity, as some project, then those less shackled by conventional ways of doing things and less socialized for a common collective identity will probably benefit more than those who are prisoners of their class."

In that last sentence the authors should have included the word *change*. Transforming change not only is more certain than prosperity, but when it has already shattered the accepted mores of even such Establishment bastions as AT&T, that's evidence enough of a Big Bang birth of a drastically different kind of economy where boardroom jobs and other rewards go to the boldly creative rather than to the well connected. There is some evidence on this point in Chapter 8.

It is interesting to note that these elite boarding schools are predominantly Episcopalian (because Anglophile Easterners copied the English and were among the first to set up private schools), and that while Episcopalians account for only 2 percent of the population, about 33 percent of the Fortune 500 corporations were headed by Episcopalians in 1950. But today the story is dramatically different. The 1986 Fortune survey showed that Catholics held 19.1 percent of those chief executive titles. Only 17.6 percent were Episcopalians.

This doesn't mean the elite schools have been heavily infil-trated by Catholics, who have established several good ones of their own in this century. However, the elite schools in recent decades have let down the bars to admit Jews and other non-WASPS. In short, like the nation, their population is more di-versified now. What the shift does reflect is a changing world.

It is a pretty safe bet that the roster of colleges producing these leaders as well as those in many other fields has shown a comparable shift. All one has to do is check out some of the indicators of college quality such as those in Chapter 8. So it follows that if a school has a famous name but doesn't help prepare one for the bold leap or the innovative approach, doesn't develop critical analytical and communicating abilities, or doesn't open minds or affect values, it will have been a liability and not just a disappointment in a frontier economy or in any vigorous, growing one.

As John L. Munschauer, director of Cornell University's ca-reer development service, wrote in *The Chronicle of Higher Education* describing the kind of student employers are scour-ing the country to find: "If what comes through are the ability to do difficult mental work, an open mind with intellectual and cultural interest and curiosity, and a mature attitude, then I have found [that kind]."

The experience of one young Beloit graduate has more than fit her to his description. She said, "I came from a little town in central Kansas where no one is going anywhere and where they all have a limited outlook. If I had gone to Kansas U. I would have joined a sorority and married a banker. My friends did go to Kansas, are back home, and are conservatives. They have not been stretched. My college experience was a window to the world. Beloit opened those windows and doors. It made me politically aware. It exposed me to new life-styles and cul-tures. It made me see the active citizen as a normal thing. Beloit showed me options. Beloit challenged people to look at their values. It forced me to confront my values in an honest way, especially in an ethics class with kids of radically different views. It channeled my religious interest into concern for the world. I had to write a personal statement on my values, which made me question and understand my values for the first time. I was challenged both in and out of the classroom."

After graduation she spent eight years in Guatemala in a Peace Corps nutrition project. But first she had to find a way to teach the Mayan Indians Spanish so she could help them. They knew no Spanish, she knew no Mayan, and there was no body of written Mayan to start from. So she found linguists to codify the parts of speech and grammar. Then she set up and staffed a school. She now has a Master of Business Administration degree from Harvard, and Beloit has named her to its board of trustees.

The son of a newspaper editor in Los Angeles who was interested principally in rebuilding cars when I met him telephoned me four years later to say, "When I came to you I had no idea I could hack it in college. The first year I didn't particularly like it [Cornell College in Iowa], but by my senior year I thought it was wonderful, and I've just been accepted for a Ph.D. program. It turned me on."

The son of a doctor in a Washington suburb had a similar awakening at Ohio Wesleyan. In the spring of his senior year in high school he wanted to drop out. I persuaded him to stick it out for the couple of months left of the term. Eight years later I got a call from him saying he'd just gotten a Ph.D. in geology. At college he'd had teachers who cared both about teaching and the kids they were teaching and who got him involved.

Parents, who deserve the blame for much of the pressure to study business or some other job-oriented curriculum, are, as they say of generals, fighting the last war, the college career advisers warn. Such graduates might be qualified for some specific entry-level task, but when time comes for promotion, they don't have what it takes. They lack people skills; they don't know how to learn, they can't handle a wide range of responsibilities, and as the head of a New Jersey state program said, the companies find "they're not management material."

The ideal future executive, according to these advisers, might be a young woman who had considered Dartmouth, tried Emory for a year, and transferred to Antioch. She wrote to me:

> It wasn't "college" that affected me. It was the *whole Antioch experience* (which includes the co-op experiences, our sense of community with its supportive and caring atmosphere, and our highly individualized and personalized academic program) that affected me. Therefore, rather than ask, "How did college affect you?" a better question might be, "How did the Antioch experience affect you?"
>
> My response: It taught me to think. At Antioch I learned how to learn. I have developed a strong sense of confidence in myself. I know I could arrive anywhere in the world: Kenya, Turkey, Japan and not know the language, but I'd survive. In fact, I'd do more than survive. I'd most likely learn the language and immerse myself in that culture for a while. Hopefully I'd become a productive member of that community during my stay.
>
> The Antioch experience has affected my values in all sorts of ways. It has made me more tolerant, more open to the idea that there are different truths other than the American ideal. I've grown tremendously since I enrolled at Antioch. Once an Antiochan, you are really affected for life.

The carry-over effect is the hallmark of the experience that powerfully affects, as this 1981 letter attests. The writer has a better job now but her letter would read much the same if written today. It said:

> Going to Eckerd was a delightful experience—one, needless to say—I will never forget—and I feel confident that my education was as good as can be found anywhere in this country. (Actually, I shouldn't be talking about it in the past tense: Eckerd taught me, among other things, that education never stops.) During my four years there I met such a wide variety of people and ideas as I had never known existed, and found the world to be a wonderfully big place.
>
> Now, as you can see, I'm working in my chosen profession of

publishing. I've been an editorial assistant since last April and hope to be an editor in a year or so. I'm getting married this year to a person I met while studying under Eckerd's auspices in London (every student should take advantage of that program, which is excellent). And I am still in contact with three or four of my former professors and many of my former classmates. Again, thank you for guiding me to a path which has always been provocative and never easy or dull.

Another woman, who was a dean at Brown before becoming one at Maryland, and who feels as ardently about Grinnell, supplied this note: "I've got Ivy League friends who are incredulous that several of us in my class still have a round-robin letter going to discuss the books we've been reading and current topics we think are important." They find it hard to believe on all three counts: that any such group of alums is doing that much reading, and that they're going to the trouble of writing letters to disuss both it and the concerns of the world.

Two sisters who hold significant jobs have some strong myth-dispelling views on whether the prestige school helps one's career more than the little-known good college. One woman is executive director of the Investor Responsibility Research Center, which provides information on which universities, colleges, and other institutions can base enlightened investment policies. She gives Lawrence University in Wisconsin much credit for continuing her education and providing useful leadership throughout her career. She contrasts her postgraduate experience with that of her Radcliffe sister, a key manager at IBM, whose ties to Radcliffe have all but disappeared through the years. "Both of us had fruitful years in college," she says, "and certainly having Radcliffe on her resume hasn't hurt a bit. But Radcliffe has not noticed her and singled her out and reached out to make new opportunities for her the way Lawrence has for me."

A senior editor of a major national publication says fifteen years afterward:

My experience at Reed is still affecting me. It affects the way I look
at things, the way I think, and my values. I cannot refuse to hear
out another opinion, the other side, however much I might dislike
it. I think that is common to any Reed graduate; whatever his or
her views, he will be fair. A Harvard graduate I know does not feel
this way. He has The Word. Also, I do not take it as an attack when
someone questions my position or my argument. To me, an attack
on a viewpoint is an intellectual probing, not an ad hominem. I
have three friends with backgrounds very similar to mine who went
to large public and private universities and all three will take a
questioning as an attack. I feel a responsibility to go on learning,
and while they also do go on learning, with me it's an imperative.
Similarly, I feel an active concern for the common welfare rather
than a passive, wait-to-be-confronted kind of social responsibility.
My college experience affected my values by what I think is important and by making it impossible for me not to have intellectual
integrity. And I don't think you could have that and not have moral
integrity.

A large star in the American clerical firmament is Pinckney
C. Enniss, minister of the Central Presbyterian Church in Atlanta, who was given an honorary doctorate by Davidson, his
alma mater, in recognition of his achievements in making Atlanta a better and more caring place. In college he had no
thought of becoming a minister; that came in full maturity and
after he had served in the Korean War. "I was a hell-raiser when
I was here," he said.

Even so, the college experience penetrated, for what he has
to say has a familiar ring:

There are few specific college courses, lectures, textbooks, or laboratories that I can point to as having prepared me for a career in
ministry. It was much more the atmosphere, the openness of the
campus environment which encouraged an appetite for learning,
allowing for questioning and pushing us toward a search for meaning, value, and truth. I would have been the last to recognize it at
the time, but looking back, I think I am most indebted to my liberal
arts college for what must be the liberal arts consensus. Some-

where, somehow, without even being aware, I was gaining a sense of the sacredness of creation and of all those who inhabit creation. For the gift of such an "awakening" I shall forever be grateful to the liberal arts tradition.

Neither the hell-raiser nor any of the others has a word to say about the college finding the first job or a career-oriented program helping them. But it made them better. As Eddie Stanky, the St. Louis Cardinal infielder who was voted the National League's Most Valuable Player one year although he was neither a leading hitter or fielder, said, "It's my intangibles."

In view of all this it is hardly surprising that every study, every indicator, says the wise thing is to go to a place and take courses with teachers that may bring out your special qualities. When men and women in mid-life are asked to look back on their college experiences, in overwhelming numbers they say, like Dr. Enniss, that what they remember are the values, the standards, the stimulus to continue developing themselves. Most of the course content has been forgotten.

Employers of all kinds—state, Federal, and private—have confirmed what the old grads say. When the job market was bad in the late seventies, several liberal arts colleges got Federal or foundation grants to find out what would make their graduates attractive to employers. What they found was that employers uniformly were much more interested in the applicant's ability to think and to communicate, as revealed by his or her ability to write a coherent paragraph or resume or to conduct a sensible, grammatical interview, than in his major, his grades, or the name of his college. Equally important were the human qualities; the ability to obtain the cooperation and the respect of others. Indeed, one faculty team wrote that they were "astonished to discover" that these things were more important than the applicant's academic background, the reputation of the college or university, personal connections, or even grades.

This discovery of a new set of ground rules in the job market echoed in part those of a Haverford psychology professor, Dr.

Douglas Heath, who for over thirty-five years has been studying the effects of that rigorous Quaker college on its graduates. It is a surpassingly successful group and the principal influence on their development has been their undergraduate college. And the outstanding quality of these men (the first class of women, at this writing, has only been out five years), as rated by their professional colleagues, has been their ethical integrity.

Although it is now being brought out of the closet, for many years the word *moral* has been shunned by students as well as faculty, even though all the crucial decisions of life are subjective value judgments, not cool cerebrations of pure, trained reason.

The alumni of Haverford—like those of many other good colleges—have long been testifying that *moral* is the central word and that the good small college is the one most likely to be the blinding light on the road to Damascus.

This group provides unusually good evidence: Over 80 percent of them have advanced degrees, whether in medicine, law, business management, engineering, social work, or one of the academic disciplines. Over 20 percent of them have taught in major colleges and universities. Over 40 percent have secured patents, published books, articles, or poems, and many have received post-college awards. Several were presidents or managers of their firms.

The Haverford alumni said their graduate or professional schools did little or nothing to help them develop the qualities of character that contributed to their success. Only one lawyer spoke of a course in law school that examined ethical values. And, Dr. Heath noted, "Although the majority of them were being educated to serve others, only one said his professional school reinforced his desire to serve them."

Dr. Heath's findings hit him hard enough to make him change his whole mode and emphasis in teaching his own courses at Haverford. His research also confirms what Philip Jacob of the University of Pennsylvania reported thirty years ago in *Changing Values in College*. Dr. Jacob said that teachers and institutions that set high standards for themselves, who critically examine their own values and expect the same from their students, do influence their intellectual and moral development. However, relatively few teachers or institutions do this.

Indeed, Dr. Heath said that at his own alma mater (Amherst), "I was seldom challenged by the faculty or the college's ethos to confront self-consciously my own values; I received an excellent intellectual education but I was not much affected by the college." An education that "does not work itself into a man's values, challenge his view of himself, and alter his relations with others, is unlikely to produce many maturing effects that persist," he added.

The years 1988 and 1989 might be considered notable for two reasons: one, the government started taking official notice of the greenhouse effect of atmospheric pollution on the planet, and two, there is an increased awareness of *moral* values. For the first time since Woodrow Wilson's address in 1902, a new Princeton president, Harold Shapiro, dealt with moral values in his installation address. He said that giving students the ability and desire to engage in the moral discourse required to give meaning to our national life was the university's most important job. But most universities fail to do this. As sociologist Robert Bellah and other researchers have concluded, with a few exceptions the university is a place where one goes to fulfill his private dreams of individual success. It does not develop these moral values.

If there were any Heath-like research to discover whether name or prestige contributes as much to success as a school's ethos, the findings undoubtedly would be startling. A lot of little-known colleges would be found equaling or outperforming many well-known ones.

As the data in the preceding chapter demonstrate, many schools that are barely or not at all selective consistently outperform some of the top research universities in the production of scholars and scientists. And a search of people distinguished enough to be listed in the 1988–1989 edition of *Who's Who* shows they outdo not only many of the leading research universities but many of the prestige colleges as well. And they have been doing so for decades, despite the fact that many of them don't have the luxury of picking only the best high school students to work with.

As Dr. Heath says, it is the quality of the experience, not the name of it, that is the key.

Especially in a swiftly changing, growing economy, the personal qualities the college has developed are the critical factors. Four years of college can't make anyone a practitioner in any field that isn't routine or formulaic, and as alumni all testify, when surveyed, the course content has evaporated anyway. And today, more than ever, no one has a crystal ball clear enough to see the career landscape even ten years hence. Dental schools are retrenching or closing. Teaching certificates once were gilt-edged. Other popular fields may become overcrowded or even obsolete. Engineering has its swings from feast to famine, and when it's famine these specialists can't adapt to a changing job market as easily as the generalists who have developed the mental agility to adapt. Furthermore, engineers—like other specialists—need nonspecialist savvy as they move up, like dealing with people.

A good many years ago, before Saudi Arabia seized the American oil companies, the head of ARAMCO and his son were discussing his college program with me when his son protested, "If I'm going to be an engineer, why do I need all this liberal arts stuff?" To which his father responded, "Because engineers who know only engineering remain engineers."

AT&T a few years ago did a self-study that goes the father one better. That giant technical corporation dominated by engineers wanted to find out if a liberal arts graduate could survive there. He does, and very well, thank you. While only 10 percent of AT&T's employees have liberal arts degrees, 43 percent of them achieved at least the fourth level of management—a measure of considerable success. Only 23 percent of the engineers did as well.

"We discovered," said company spokesman Burke Stinson, "that in the managing of a business the liberal arts people were not wedded to a particular idea or approach; they were open; they were more creative. A linear manager [translate: engineer] would try to fit a problem into a specific box. The engineer felt comfortable with a small group of likes, but when he expanded his scope, his comfort dropped. The nonlinear executive did a better job of communicating; the engineer was more militaristic; the nonlinear executive was more receptive.

"The future is to the creative, the leap-taker. An engineering company is no longer limited to engineers. It is influenced by what happens today in Korea or Königsberg. It is very different from the old days."

The familial college that compels the youth to do the kind of internal and external exploration that affects the development of values and sharpens and enlightens the mind is the one most likely to develop the creative, the leap-taker for the future. And whatever its name, that kind of college will pay the richest lifelong dividends.

An Important Feminist Note

In a university administrative group meeting in the sixties to discuss scholarship policies, the chancellor suggested giving them only to men because the women would just get married and have families. "Like Mrs. Compton," I said, "whose three sons were presidents of MIT, the University of Washington, and Washington University, and one of whom was a Nobel Prize winner, not to mention a lawyer daughter distinguished enough to get an honorary doctorate of laws." The suggestion was dropped.

That attitude may be no longer prevalent but the incident illustrates one of the reasons I've always believed the education of a girl to be more important than that of a boy. Her planning should be less influenced by current fashion; it should be at least as long-range and basic as that of her brother because her life is likely to involve more variables than his. Her education should make her versatile, give her room for growth and future maneuver. Why?

First, because the probabilities today are greater than ever that she will start a career, interrupt it for several months to several years while she has a child or is at home with children, maybe even until they're in high school, and then go back to work. While she's out both the job market and her interests may change. It seems to me that not only are nearly all of the well-off mothers I talk to working outside the home, but also that they are doing things they would never have guessed they'd be doing when they were in college.

The Census Bureau supports me in this. It has now certified that the working mother has become a way of life. In 1987, for the first time, more than half of the nation's new mothers remained in the job market or returned within a year. For mothers with college degrees the figure was 63 percent. The Bureau did not offer any figures on what percentage returned after several years, but noted that two thirds of the widowed, divorced, or separated mothers were working. It also said that in more than 40 percent of all families in the childbearing ages of eighteen to forty-four, both parents worked.

The second and more important reason is that, like Mrs. Compton, the mother is the source of comfort, the day-long standard-setter, and the principal influence on the character and the aspirations of the next generation. Q.E.D.

10 🔊
A Few Favorites and Two Hundred Worth Going To

Colleges That Have Helped Kids of All Kinds

Once, several years ago, I was getting nowhere trying to persuade a young client that all wasn't going to be lost just because he couldn't get into an Ivy League school for which he didn't have the credentials anyway. With some hyperbole I assured him that some of the dumbest people of my own vintage I knew had gone to Princeton. With a hint of a sigh his mother joined in with, "Yes, that's where my husband went." Between us, we had given him the message (whether he heard it or not) that is central to this book because it is so true: that the name of the college doesn't do the job.

Like most other people, I have known quite a number of adults who have little more to brag about in their lives than where they went to college, but I have known still more who went to no-name colleges who are their betters, and are sometimes their bosses to boot. And this is as good a place as any to make a statement that needs to be shouted from the rooftops:

admissions directors and their committees have very cloudy crystal balls and seriously flawed criteria for their decisions. In my experience, Harvard, Wharton School of the University of Pennsylvania, and Cornell, among other very selective schools, have accepted second-rate human beings with good records and rejected first-rate ones whose academic numbers were less impressive.

In one such case, Amherst's alumni interviewer said an outstanding youngster was doing too many things. The Princeton admissions officer said he wouldn't be able to handle the verbal demands because his SAT verbal score was only 440. Nevertheless, he had a 3.95 average in a tough program at a most competitive suburban high school, wrestled at 120 pounds instead of his normal 140 by dint of pushing himself away from the table, lettered in cross country three years, was junior class president, and was cited for his work on a county committee on high school counseling. He also kept the TV set turned off "for 102 days." His English teacher said his ideas were almost always the best in the class but not his writing, so he added a writing course to his agenda. For a summer's archaeology dig he got four hours' credit from the University of Wisconsin. In a solo project for a county historical commission, he did the research, then discovered, mapped, and wrote a report on what had been a pre-Revolutionary fortified outpost on the Potomac River. Four years after the Princeton officer doubted he could handle the challenge, he graduated from Vassar—where the demands are no less difficult—with a 3.6 average.

Both Princeton's and William and Mary's crystal balls were even murkier when they rejected a young friend who had zipped through high school in three years. She chose Hampshire but discovered after two years it was not for her and transferred to the University of Virginia where she graduated Phi Beta Kappa and later got a Master's with Distinction. Now she is getting her Ph.D. in English literature from the university and English department ranked number one in the nation, the University of California at Berkeley. Furthermore, Berkeley gave her a fellowship she didn't even apply for, and she's had a scholarly article published.

(Harvard, however, should get a nod for resisting influence. A young client, son of a Washington power figure, was both a Yale and a Harvard legacy for more than two generations back, but his high school record wouldn't have gotten anyone else into any Ivy or Little Ivy school. The Harvard admissions officer said, "We know he's got friends in high places, but he's not going to walk in here." And he didn't, though Yale opened the door for him.)

There is no correlation, except for mathematicians, between grade point averages in school and achievement in life. A foundation-supported study of thirty years ago found this was the case, as old grads often brag. Mathematicians are an exception because they are born and not made. Furthermore, as you'll see in Chapter 12, surveys of alumni have shown the top students to be the least happy adults. But admissions directors, to protect the image of the product they're selling—and for no other reason—insist on a 600 verbal score if they have the luxury of many applicants. Such a criterion, however, is worse than voodoo economics. Status, not service, is god. Furthermore, some colleges falsify their freshman profiles by not including the scores and class ranks of legacies, minorities, or those on athletic "scholarships." In fact, at a professional meeting one admissions officer was quoted as justifying excluding all the low scores by saying, "That's not our profile."

I have never had a former client or anyone else tell me how a great university or an Ivy school had changed him or her. On the contrary, parents have occasionally reported something like: "Carol isn't going back to Michigan. She says that everything you told her about it is true." I had expressed my usual reservations about graduate-assistant teaching, big classes, impersonality, distant professors, and lack of involvement in a student's education. The daughter transferred to one of the colleges we had discussed. And one who went to Penn said the same things.

The other side of the coin is that a parent or recent graduate has often taken the trouble to let me know how much some little-known college has helped. In one such case where I had been suggesting places the family had never heard of, the mother finally demanded, "Mr. Pope, what would you be suggesting if this was your daughter?" My reply, "I treat them all that way," satisfied her for the moment, but what four years at Guilford did for the girl made them permanent Guilford enthusiasts. And later when the daughter married a former classmate, I told her mother there'd be no extra charge.

Omniscience is in as short supply here as anywhere else, and no chapter could ever do justice to all the colleges that deserve mention. What I can do is call attention to those which I have reason to believe have made a difference for the better in peoples' lives, and often a bigger difference than some exceedingly selective brand-name college might have made. Some of them are difficult to get into, some easy, and some are at various points in between; but whether they admit feeble students or strong ones, they contribute to a student's development. Usually it is the uncertain, C student who needs the nurturing more; the smart, certain one is going to get it at any good place, or he has only himself to blame.

No one should be intimidated by the categories that follow; for instance, while the Antioch graduate may be marked by a confident self-reliance and willingness to venture, a lot of high school seniors who didn't fit that description grew into it in four years there. Similarly, while St. John's tends to attract persons with high verbal scores, one of the college's claims is that the ones with modest scores will benefit just as much; indeed, that has always been the conviction of the Great Books advocates. So, with that emphatic caveat, here is my list of favorites.

For Those Who Can March to a Different Drummer

Antioch in Ohio has to be in a paragraph by itself. A pioneer in experiential education, it appeals to persons willing to march to a different drummer and it gives them an intensely personal education in a caring and supportive atmosphere. The student has to assume some responsibility for his own education. The co-op work experiences not only contribute to the educating and maturing of the youth, but also produce a college student body as independent and self-sufficient as any on the face of the earth; having had an intellectual Outward Bound experience, they are fully confident of themselves, and with good reason.

Few colleges have made greater contributions to the common good than Antioch, and none is more tolerant of the prickly personality or the unpopular viewpoint. Indeed, when students were trashing the campus in the early seventies because they hated President Nixon, I felt the then-administration was so open-minded that its brains had fallen out. Antioch has had four financial crises in this century, the last one in the late seventies seemingly life-threatening; but had the crisis been severe enough, some foundation surely would have come to the rescue, simply because the country cannot afford not to have an Antioch.

And, although it has been selective only two or three years in its life, it ranks about midway in the top fifty-nine colleges whose graduates get into *Who's Who*.

For the Self-Sufficient Self-Starter

Evergreen   Marlboro
Hampshire   New College of the U. of South Florida

Evergreen in Washington is the great public academic bargain in the Northwest, while Hampshire in Massachusetts and Marlboro in Vermont are the outstanding academic bargains in the Northeast, and New in the Southeast, although only a small percentage of teenagers would find any one of them suitable. Each demands that the student be able to plan ahead and work on his own, something few do at that stage of life. At Marlboro, since there are only two hundred students and thirty-five faculty members in a pastoral Vermont setting, one must also be socially self-sufficient. Hampshire is in a class by itself for the enterprising student who wants a larger, more urban, Grade A New England college with access to classes at Amherst, Mount Holyoke, Smith, and the University of Massachusetts. The applicant with reasonably good grades will probably get in if the admissions office thinks it's a good match.

New College is not that kind of bargain; it accepts less than half of its applicants, who are intellectuals rather than grade-grubbers. Like the other three, it expects the student to be heavily involved in the planning and execution of his own program. It is a bargain for the serious student.

For the Pure Intellectuals

Reed
St. John's, in Annapolis, Maryland, and Santa Fe, New Mexico.

These are bargains for the person who reads good stuff and is interested in ideas, although in the 1987 and 1988 applications surges Reed became more selective than it had been. Neither gives grades, although Reed records them. Reed has a core program required of all students; St. John's is all core: the (hundred) Great Books of Western civilization, plus four years each of math, science, and language. The purpose of the language—two years of Greek and two of French—is not to learn them, but to learn to think in English. St. John's students also take two years of music because it is a form of communication. There are no majors, but a high percentage of seniors goes on to graduate and professional schools. As one St. John's student put it, "We spend four years discussing 'What is truth?' " Others see it as a very practical program. A future artist found it the most intensely active learning community of any college she'd visited, and the kind of preparation any kind of artist needed. And a faculty member at Lewis and Clark, a Portland neighbor of Reed, observed with academic sour grapes, "Their [Reed's] faculty isn't all that good; they just get kids with a commitment to learning."

For a Humanities Student

Johns Hopkins
University of Rochester

The serious student, especially the future Ph.D., who is passionately in love with literature or some other non-science subject, will be in small classes and should have good rapport with at least some of the renowned scholars on the Hopkins faculty. Hopkins is exceedingly selective for science students since it attracts a lot more of them than it needs. But it's a different ballgame for the humanities students, which Hopkins wants more of. Hence, for them it is far and away the greatest bargain on the East Coast, if the lure of scholarly association outweighs the disadvantages of a university.

Rochester's new president is trying to give a place that, like Hopkins, is heavy on science and engineering the look and feel of a liberal arts college. Faculty-student rapport has been made a priority; there are exchanges of professors with other institutions; and Wednesday afternoon is class-free, so students can attend special exhibits or events or just do their laundry. And a few students can have a tuition-free fifth year to expand their horizons beyond their specialties. Because Rochester is trying to build a more diversified, national student body, it will represent a first-rate academic bargain for the humanities or social science student at least for the next few years.

NOTE
All four of these groups are communities where there's not likely to be a middle ground; it's likely to be either a love affair or disaffection. Hampshire is a dramatic example; its image has suffered because the publicity its novel program received

when it opened in 1970 lured too many teenagers who didn't do their consumer research or their self-examination and who found they couldn't handle the responsibility.

Four Brand-Name Best Buys

Four brand-name colleges that don't qualify as admissions bargains nevertheless belong here because they have made as much a difference in peoples' lives as any. They are:

> Bryn Mawr   Oberlin
> Haverford   Swarthmore

Proportional to their size, no four institutions have made greater contributions to our society than these. And while Bryn Mawr, Haverford, and Swarthmore are as selective as any Ivy school, all four are alternatives to Ivies that are likely to have much more impact on a young mind and conscience.

Haverford and Swarthmore both reflect their Quaker origins with their emphasis on the individual's responsibility for seeking and applying truth and an ethical concern for the duties of human beings. Haverford students live by an honor code; Swarthmore pioneered the honors program, in which students work on their own or closely with faculty members the last two years. Haverford, having in recent years gone coed, is still more of a men's school. Haverford also has, in the opinion of one young Swarthmore alumna who took a class there, more of the Quaker influence, a sense of simplicity and, as its own students testify, of trust. Haverford is smaller, is more homogeneous, upper middle class, and has more sense of community, but by the same token, it has smaller departments than Swarthmore, which has engineering and a considerably more diverse student body.

Bryn Mawr, also of Quaker origin and a sister school to Haverford, has always had the reputation of being the most intellectual of the top women's colleges. In fact, a young woman once complained to me, "I'm the only person on campus who doesn't have her eye on her Ph.D. dissertation."

Oberlin not only shares the others' emphasis on intellectual growth, but it is marked by a greater sense of social responsibility, something that is part of its history. In 1835, two years after it opened, the trustees declared that "the education of people of color is a matter of great interest and should be encouraged and sustained in this institution." Before the Civil War it was a part of the Underground Railway for slaves fleeing to freedom. By the turn of the century, one third of all black graduates of white institutions were Oberlin graduates. Nor did it discriminate against Jews or women, and the first three women in America to get the bachelor's degree graduated in 1841. It is in character, therefore, that one is likely to hear more conversation about society's problems and injustices at Oberlin than at the others. Its alumni are more apt to be philosophers, professors, writers, government officials, or head of some good work than bank or corporation presidents, although they have their share of those too. Oberlin's absolutely peerless music conservatory is justly famous, and it has the best college art museum as well as an art history department without peer.

If the college world had not abandoned quotas, City College of New York, now a unit of the City University of New York, would be listed with the four above. For decades, CCNY, one of the few places that did not discriminate against Jews, offered an open door to countless poor youths who have since made incomparable contributions to the nation, besides producing seven Nobel laureates compared to mighty Harvard's nine. All seven now add luster to Harvard's faculty. The long discrimination against Jews at other colleges, although much worse than that now claimed against Asians, had at least one refrain in common. An Ivy admissions officer in those days told me, with some exaggeration, "If I didn't discriminate, my class would be ninety-seven percent Jewish."

The Best Buys for a Wide Range of Abilities

The next couple of dozen are some of the most attractive admissions bargains in the land because they are open to students of a wide range of abilities. Their student bodies include top-notch as well as C+ students, and occasionally some of the just plain C variety. Their faculties not only are as first rate as any, but what is more important, they care about their students. At most of them, at least half the students will have spent an off-campus study term in this country or abroad. All are places where one will get a better education than at most prestige universities. They are:

Austin	Kenyon
Bard	Knox
Beloit	Lawrence
Centre	Macalester
Cornell College	Ohio Wesleyan
Denison	Pitzer
Eckerd	Ripon
Earlham	Rhodes
Grinnell	St. Andrews
Hampden-Sydney	St. Olaf
Hiram	South, U. of the
Hobart and William Smith	Wabash
Kalamazoo	Wooster

Austin is a school of high standards that would be very selective if it were located in one of the heavily populated areas of the country. Its only drawback is that nearly everybody's from Texas.

Bard, up the Hudson from New York City, is very small, with one of the country's best college presidents and an intellectually alive, nonconformist community. It ranks among the top fifty-nine institutions in the percentage of alumni in the 1988–1989 edition of *Who's Who*. If it's on your wavelength, you won't do better. And if you're one of the top ten in a public high school, tuition won't be more than your state university's.

Beloit, ninety miles from Chicago in Wisconsin, is one of the best quality buys in the country. It is another of the top fifty. Also, it has a national, very diverse student body and is a happy, familial community. On a visit there I was having so much trouble trying to elicit some gripes about the place that in mid-afternoon a boy approached me conspiratorially and offered, "I understand you're trying to find out bad things about Beloit." It turned out he didn't like his political science prof.

Centre in Kentucky, like Austin in Texas, is a regional school and a very good one.

Cornell College in Iowa, named for Ezra, who gave his money to the other one, is another excellent, albeit largely regional, college, and another at the top of the *Who's Who* list. It has been a place that produces a disproportionately large share of writers, scholars, and executives.

Denison has a well-to-do student body, an excellent faculty, a distinguished record of producing scholars and scientists, and no prettier campus anywhere.

Eckerd in Florida, although only in its youth, has already established itself as a very desirable place with a diversified student body and as a place that has an impact; witness the fact that it's one of the high producers of future Ph.D.'s.

Earlham in Indiana is simply one of the best undergraduate colleges anywhere. While it is a Quaker school it often has more Catholics, Jews, or Methodists than Quakers in its freshman class. Not only does it affect mental and moral development, it is a caring, warm, supportive place. Just as much as Antioch, but in a different way, it is the kind of college a democracy can't have too many of.

Grinnell in Iowa is also a school that has a demonstrable impact, and is another top *Who's Who* producer. No New England or California college is better; few are as good. Indeed, the intellectual adventure at Grinnell is livelier, and the diversity probably greater, since only one sixth of the students come from Iowa, over a quarter are Jewish, and they come from all parts of the country and the world.

Hampden-Sydney in Virginia, one of two liberal arts men's schools left, is one that on the basis of quality should be deluged with applicants. It too is one of the *Who's Who* stars.

Hiram in Ohio is a solidly good college that has turned on many a young friend of mine and is now getting more selective as a consequence of success.

Hobart and William Smith in upstate New York constitute a high quality, imaginative, slightly preppy, regional twin college easier to get into but every bit as good as a lot of the most selective ones.

Kalamazoo in that Michigan city is another gem that, if sited in New England, would be terribly tough to get into, but which like several other Midwest ones is better than most Eastern schools. Furthermore, Kalamazoo is more attractive and more alive than any Eastern or Western city of anywhere near the same size. It was the first to create pedestrian malls, and it has more outstanding residential architecture—by Frank Lloyd Wright, Alden Dow, and Norman Carver—than any city a great deal larger.

Kenyon, in lovely little Gambier, Ohio, is another that is far superior to most Eastern colleges more difficult to get into, as its performance in the *Who's Who* canvas shows. As author E. L. Doctorow was quoted in *The New York Times* as saying, "We did with poetry at Kenyon what they did with football at Ohio State."

Knox in Illinois, like Kalamazoo, is a first rater that would be deluged with applicants if people weren't so provincial. Its studio art facilities are more extensive than at any college I've seen.

Lawrence in Wisconsin, like Grinnell, has few peers, although it has less diversity than Beloit or Grinnell.

Macalester, in Minnesota, which has suddenly gotten very warm, if not hot, and in 1988 rejected at least one kid with a 3.4 average, is also first rate, though a little lower on my pecking order than some of those already mentioned, because as at Brown, kids have the freedom to get out without a liberal education. The only course requirements are one in social sciences, one in mathematics or a science, and two in humanities or fine arts. Twenty years ago, thanks to the largesse of the *Reader's Digest* owners, it had more National Merit Scholars than any college in the land.

Ohio Wesleyan is another Midwest scorer in *Who's Who* that has a much more diverse, cosmopolitan, and friendlier student body and better faculty than a lot of the more selective East and West Coast schools.

Pitzer in California, the newest of the Claremont Colleges—the Little Ivies of the West Coast—and the least difficult to get into, is the only college in the country to make its major emphasis the social and behavioral sciences. Not surprisingly, students have to assume some responsibility for their own education, and for campus governance as well.

Ripon in Wisconsin is a venerable, good, conservative college. If it were in the East, it'd be called preppy. It also profits from being one of the Associated Colleges of the Midwest, which have an unmatched array of foreign and domestic off-campus.programs.

Rhodes is a place that made a deep impression on me at least fifteen years ago, when it was Southwestern at Memphis. When the black students in Northern and Midwestern schools were segregating themselves, on this Deep South campus they told me they were full and happy participating members of the community. And it is a community with a vigorous intellectual tradition, partly because for many it is a preprofessional school.

St. Andrews in North Carolina, and others like it, play an essential role in the collegiate scheme. It has nurtured, broadened, and strengthened many a young person with a fragile self-image or modest grades who would have been lucky to have had such an experience otherwise. An Ivy school alumnus, when telling me about his son who didn't have Ivy League credentials, said that nevertheless everything turned out well because "we found this great little college in North Carolina that did wonders for him." I knew without being told he was talking about St. Andrews; so many of my clients have said the same thing.

St. Olaf in Minnesota is an exceptional place, and with Wooster, one of the two best-kept secrets in higher education simply because it has never made an effort to attract a nationwide applicant pool rather than a predominantly Midwest Lutheran one. Its faculty is superb; indeed, its math department is as good as any in the country, even Dartmouth's. Its choir is famous, its kids are the kind you'd like yours to be. Out of curiosity I went to church on a visit there, and out of a student population of three thousand, there must have been a thousand at the service.

University of the South, known as Sewanee, in Tennessee, is also a high quality school, as its record in turning out people who get into *Who's Who* shows. Its students are mainly Southern and conservative.

Wabash in Indiana, the other liberal arts men's college and *Who's Who* star, is first rate in every respect. As a producer of scholars, scientists, and other achievers, this college of eight hundred makes some of the Ivies and prestige colleges look sick. Furthermore, it is a place to check out if you are a good student and want a scholarship. Wabash probably has a higher percentage of students on no-need aid than any other college, due largely to the generosity of Eli Lilly.

Wooster in Ohio is the other best-kept secret and one of the best academic bargains in the country. It is also among the *Who's Who* fifty-nine. Until about twenty-five years ago it not only was WASP, but Presbyterian WASP. No effort was made to attract a diverse clientele until the college boom got under way. (Now it has a rabbi working with its Jewish students.) Also, it was so well financed that faculty didn't have to compete in any national marketplace for research grants. Its only visibility was in the academic world, which knew of its graduates' achievements. These accomplishments have been remarkable, especially considering that Wooster never was selective and didn't busily seek out the high school valedictorians. Nevertheless, as noted elsewhere, it ranks eleventh among all the colleges in the production of future Ph.D.'s. Also, more faculty in the twelve Great Lakes Colleges Association send their children to Wooster than to any of the others.

As the statistics in Chapter 8 show, several of these colleges are as distinguished as any college, and much more so than most universities, when judged by their fruit. More to the point, they may be much more potent forces in a youth's development. At any of these the student will have better *teachers* and far more contact with them than at the most famous universities. The other half of the bargain is that the doors are open to applicants the famous ones wouldn't look at.

For Late Bloomers or Those Who Need Help

Curry	Misericordia
Landmark*	Montreat-Anderson†
Davis & Elkins	St. Andrews
Dean† .	West Virginia Wesleyan
Mitchell†	

†—Junior colleges.
*—A pre-college and two-year college for the learning disabled.

To paraphrase what Lincoln is reputed to have said of the poor, the Lord must have loved C students because he made so many of them. But many of them have been notable achievers: Ralph Waldo Emerson was supposed to have been a C student at Harvard, and President Truman was no classroom whiz. Some of the colleges on this list—Curry near Boston, Davis and Elkins in West Virginia, Dean in Massachusetts, Mitchell in Connecticut, and West Virginia Wesleyan—have formal programs to help kids with learning problems. And they do help them. Those at Curry and Mitchell especially are highly professional enterprises, as is the one at Misericordia, a Catholic college in Pennsylvania. Landmark, which opened in 1985 on the campus of defunct Windham College in Vermont, works only with dyslexics and other learning-disabled students. It has a pre-college program to enable students to handle college work, and it also offers a two-year degree in general studies.

The four-year colleges have students of a range of abilities and are also places where an underachiever can get a chance and have a successful and productive experience in a good learning experience. St. Andrews is listed here as well as above because while it has no formal program for students with learning problems and exercises care in accepting them, it nevertheless has enabled several such to have successful college experiences.

Nearly Two Hundred More Worth Going To

The list that follows is not intended to separate all the sheep from the goats. In addition to the most famous and selective are many others little known outside their locales, and much less selective or not selective at all. Many of them may be strange names but all are schools that can provide fruitful, successful experiences for youths of widely varying interests, abilities, and personalities. The intellectual who might be happy at Reed, for example, might abhor working on a ranch in the desert for twenty hours a week as part of his two years at Deep Springs. Schools of art or music or business aren't included, and the big state universities are discussed later.

In the first group are the Ivies and other very selective schools that accept half or fewer of their applicants, which means it takes high grades, a full program with honors or Advanced Placement courses, and outside accomplishments to be in the competition.

In the second group are many schools just as good, but that accept B and C+ and sometimes C students, with notations on those that might appeal to a particular kind of person.

AMHERST, which accepts one in five, epitomizes "Little Ivy," and whose admissions dean used to say, "We've been living off the rejects of Harvard, Yale, and Princeton for two hundred years and doing very well."

BARNARD, the women's college of Columbia University, takes 45 percent.

BATES takes about 40 percent, but doesn't require SATs so it is booming.

BOSTON COLLEGE, really a university, popular but no think tank.

BOWDOIN takes one in four, makes SATs optional, and one-third of acceptees don't give them.

BROWN, once the Ivies' weak sister, is now one of the most popular since it has no course requirements, which is too bad.

BUCKNELL, with a lovely campus and good students, is a place where students work for grades.

CALIFORNIA INSTITUTE OF TECHNOLOGY, the premier science school, where one recent year every freshman had scored eight hundred on the Level II math achievement test.

CALIFORNIA, U. OF, Santa Cruz, an 8,500-student cluster of small colleges and the pick of the state system for liberal arts students.

CALIFORNIA, U. OF, San Diego, also a cluster-college campus with great strength in math and the sciences. Both are public school bargains.

CARLETON, a college without peer and loaded with National Merit Scholars; also one of the top *Who's Who* scorers.

CHICAGO, U. OF, better than most Ivy universities.

CLAREMONT-MCKENNA, the political science and economics oriented of the Claremont group, where 60 percent go to graduate school.

COLGATE, only slightly less selective than the Little Ivies, with a lovely, more pastoral setting.

COLUMBIA is responsible for one of the few productive developments of higher education, the Contemporary Civilization sequence, the father of all such core curricula.

CONNECTICUT COLLEGE, a Grade A college now engaged in an important program to seek out many more black students.

COOPER UNION, a school for architecture, art, and engineering, which accepts one in five.

CORNELL U. has one of the most beautiful campuses in the country, and by reason of its many land-grant-college vocational and professional programs in addition to its arts and sciences college has a diversity not approached by any other Ivy institution.

DARTMOUTH was the first school to put a computer wired to the college's network into every student's room, the work of math whiz Dr. John Kemeny. It also has the reputation of being the most conservative Ivy school, with the smallest Jewish population, but in Dr. Kemeny it had the first Jewish president of an Ivy League school.

DAVIDSON, one of that group of which there isn't any better, is a conservative Southern school that lives by an honor code and produces achievers, as its *Who's Who* ranking indicates. Not the least of its virtues is its lovely, willow-oak shaded campus.

DEEP SPRINGS is free for the twenty-five very smart men able to take the monastic seclusion and physical demands of living on and working a farm in the California desert for two years.

DUKE became very popular in the last decade or so and is now as selective—about 21 percent accepted—as the Ivies, a situation some University of North Carolina alums attribute to "hype."

EMORY, given a $100 million gift a few years ago, the largest ever to a university, now has an endowment that enables it to suck top professors from top institutions, and its selectivity is increasing accordingly.

FRANKLIN AND MARSHALL is heavily preprofessional, and it's tougher to get in if you want to go on to business or medical school than if you want to become a teacher or a philosopher.

FURMAN is a first-rate Southern, conservative, Baptist-connected, no-liquor place.

GEORGETOWN is another school that has become very popular in the last two decades, because of its location. Its Foreign Service School and some of the big-name professors who see little of the undergraduates helped. It has a far higher percentage of non-Catholics than any other Catholic university.

HAMILTON should be classed as a bargain because it's just as good and quite a bit easier to get into than the Ivies.

HARVARD, where everybody wants to go, naturally, although most of them might be better off at any one of several of the colleges in this group, or even at some in the next.

HARVEY MUDD, the math-science member of the Claremont group, where the freshmen's mean score on the Level II math achievement one year was 790.

HOLY CROSS, along with Notre Dame and Georgetown, one of the most popular Catholic schools, with a very homogeneous student body.

LAFAYETTE is a good, conventional school, where fraternities are important.

MIAMI U., in Ohio, a public school of Ivy quality, and now nearly as hard to get into.

MASSACHUSETTS INSTITUTE OF TECHNOLOGY, for the top math, science, and engineering students.

MIDDLEBURY is another of the Grade A New England colleges, especially famed for its language programs.

MOUNT HOLYOKE, one of the best women's colleges, also has many of the advantages of a coed institution since students can take classes at any one of the others of the Five College Consortium: Amherst, University of Massachusetts, Hampshire, and Smith.

NEW YORK STATE U. at Binghamton, the academic star of the state system, a public school bargain of top quality, but has few out-of-state students.

NORTHWESTERN U., like Chicago, better than most of the Ivies.

NOTRE DAME, where academic quality is more important even than football.

OCCIDENTAL, along with the Claremont colleges, one of California's best.

POMONA, flagship of the Claremont group; the West Coast's Amherst.

PRINCETON, for embodying virtues of a college, my choice of the Ivy universities.

RENSSELAER, a top quality engineering school.

RICE, another one that's better than most of the Ivies.

ROCHESTER, where students who've overdosed on the preprofessional courses can fill in the cultural gaps with a free fifth year. Now it's a very desirable bargain.

SCRIPPS, the women's college of the Claremont group, one of the West Coast Little Ivies.

SMITH, another top women's college and a member of the Five-College group.

STANFORD, in the academic world rated above Harvard in quality.

TRINITY (Conn.), still another top quality New England school.

TUFTS students tend to be enthusiastic about their school and its quality as well as for being on the edge of Boston.

U.S. AIR FORCE ACADEMY ⎱
U.S. MILITARY ACADEMY   ⎰ for those who want military careers.
U.S. NAVAL ACADEMY   ⎰

VASSAR, another Grade A, and with Colgate, Hamilton, and Union, one of the four best colleges in New York state.

WAKE FOREST, a Grade A, conservative, Southern school with a homogeneous student body and a faculty considerably more liberal than the kids they teach.

WASHINGTON AND LEE, another first-rate, conservative community where two thirds of the students come from below the Mason-Dixon Line.

WELLESLEY, another of the best women's colleges.

WESLEYAN, one of the three Little Ivies, and the most liberal.

WILLIAMS, ditto, and the preppiest.

YALE, some prefer it to Harvard.

In the following list are schools much easier to get into:

AGNES SCOTT, an outstanding regional women's college that offers a far better education than any public and most private institutions in the state. It is in the top fifty colleges in producing future Ph.D.'s in the humanities, and one of the top 5 percent in future women Ph.D.'s in the humanities.

ALBION, a good college, where 85 percent of the students are in-staters.

ALBRIGHT, where most of the kids are from Pennsylvania; heavily preprofessional.

ALFRED is another of the top fifty, in empirical sciences.

ALLEGHENY, a high-quality school with good diversity.

ALMA, like Albion, a good school for mostly Michiganders.

ALVERNO, a women's college pioneering in weaning students from dependence on teachers. They get no grades, but must prove they've achieved competence in eight academic abilities.

AUGUSTANA (Ill.), a very good regional school.

AUGUSTANA (S.D.), a good regional, heavily preprofessional school.

BAYLOR, a firmly Southern Baptist place, heavily preprofessional.

BENNINGTON, another place for venturesome, self-motivated students only; they help design their own programs and get no grades.

BEREA, primarily for students from Appalachia.

BIRMINGHAM-SOUTHERN, a very good, very Southern, conservative school.

BRADLEY is a vocationally oriented, good regional college.

BRANDEIS, which is tougher than most of these to get into.

CALVIN (Mich.), a good regional college.

CARNEGIE-MELLON, a selective liberal arts college and four professional schools in airtight compartments.

CASE WESTERN, even though it's a university.

CLARK U., a high-quality academic bargain, a rarity in Massachusetts.

CLARKSON U., primarily an engineering school near the Adirondacks.

COE, an Iowa bargain for the C+ student.

COLBY, also very selective, conservative; lovely campus.

COLBY-SAWYER, both a two- and a four-year school.

COLORADO COLLEGE, a great faculty, good students, lovely site.

DALLAS, U. OF, a young first-rate college with diversity.

DENVER, U. OF, its great new core curriculum gives it new luster.

DEPAUW, another quality bargain and *Who's Who* producer.

DICKINSON, a very popular, fraternity-oriented school.

DREW, good faculty, very local student body.

FAIRFIELD, a Jesuit, 90 percent Catholic school; business majors everywhere.

FISK, a strong, black liberal arts college.

FORDHAM, a good Jesuit university for someone who has to go to school in New York City.

GETTYSBURG, a good school peopled by Eastern WASP fraternity and sorority members.

GODDARD, for doers concerned with social and political issues who can work on their own.

GOUCHER, a women's-college-gone-coed bargain, especially for men.

GUILFORD, a quality bargain; like Earlham, a Quaker school.

GUSTAVUS-ADOLPHUS, a very good Minnesota Lutheran school.

HAMLINE, a good local school but heavily commuter.

HAMPTON INSTITUTE, a predominantly black college that has a fine new president and new life.

HARTWICK, the C student can get in and prosper.

HOLLINS, a good women's college.

HOPE, a high producer of scientists and a good place.

HOWARD U., the top black university.

ILLINOIS INSTITUTE OF TECHNOLOGY, where one can get a good liberal education as well as architectural or scientific degrees.

ILLINOIS WESLEYAN is a serious learning place but 90 percent in-staters.

JAMES MADISON, a big, popular state institution for Virginians.

JOHN CARROLL, a solid Jesuit school but mostly commuter.

JUNIATA, long a producer of scientists.

LAKE FOREST, lovely campus, good faculty, well worth looking at.

LEHIGH, a top engineering school.

LEWIS AND CLARK, a typical Eastern or Midwest college in Oregon; mainly WASPs, beautiful campus.

LOYOLA (Md.), very good, but local.

LOYOLA (Ill.), ditto.

LUTHER has a distinguished record of producing achievers.

LYNCHBURG, once heavily Virginian, now is a bargain for C students.

MANHATTANVILLE, coed and no longer Catholic; near New York City.

MARIETTA, an Ohio bargain for the C student.

MARY WASHINGTON, one of the public bargains.

MILLS, an excellent women's college.

MILLSAPS, a very good place in Mississippi that is among the top *Who's Who* producers.

MONTEVALLO, U. OF, another public bargain.

MOREHOUSE, a top black college.

MUHLENBERG has a very regional population, most headed for medical or business school.

OGLETHORPE in Atlanta once took C students, now is more selective.

PACIFIC, U. OF, nearly three fourths Californians and no heavy pressure.

PACIFIC LUTHERAN is looking for more non-Washingtonians.

PINE MANOR, a first-rate junior college; also awards B.A.'s.

PUGET SOUND has considerable academic pressure; students are career-oriented.

RANDOLPH MACON, mostly Southern and a good school.

RANDOLPH MACON WOMAN'S COLLEGE is a serious academic place.

REDLANDS, a good, conservative WASP college with an experimental unit.

ROANOKE, a good place that will take C students.

ROLLINS, a college that's been academically bootstrapped by its president, Thad Seymour; one of Florida's best.

ST. JOHN'S U. (Minn.), one of the first Catholic colleges to make its religion department ecumenical.

SAINT LAWRENCE has a largely WASP, business-oriented clientele.

ST. MARY'S, a rare creature: a very good, small, public college in a lovely waterfront setting in southern Maryland; a financial as well as an academic bargain.

SANTA CLARA U., a high-quality small Catholic university.

SARAH LAWRENCE is one of the rare bargains in the East; for creative, motivated, and socially mature students who plan their own programs and get no grades.

SHIMER, small Illinois school that has a Great Books program.

SIMON'S ROCK, half high school, half college; a welcome solution for those who want to leave high school after the tenth or eleventh grade. An appendage of Bard College.

SKIDMORE, another college with a good new president and new life.

SOUTHERN METHODIST, now concentrating on academic quality.

SOUTHWESTERN U. (Tex.), a very good regional college.

SPELMAN, the good, predominantly black women's college that got $20 million from Bill Cosby and his wife.

SPRING HILL, a demanding Jesuit school.

STETSON, with Eckerd, Rollins, and New, one of Florida's best.

STONEHILL, a small Catholic college in Massachusetts with one third business majors.

SWEET BRIAR, a women's college; lovely campus and a good liberal education.

SYRACUSE, better than it used to be but still a big university.

THOMAS AQUINAS, a very small college with a Great Books program.

TRANSYLVANIA, in Kentucky, is well worth investigating.

TRINITY (D.C.), the oldest and perhaps the best Catholic women's college.

TRINITY U. in San Antonio, which is buying up National Merit Scholars.

TULANE, an outstanding bargain among the prestige schools.

TULSA, U. OF, has been raising its standards and recruiting more widely.

TUSKEGEE, a venerable black college.

VANDERBILT, a Southern school now getting hot in the North.

VILLANOVA, a popular heavily Catholic university.

VIRGINIA MILITARY INSTITUTE, another public bargain for those who like the military regimen. And it is one of the top *Who's Who* scorers.

WARREN WILSON, a special place; all four hundred students do fifteen hours of campus work a week as well as community service.

WASHINGTON COLLEGE, a good school now attracting a diversified student body.

WASHINGTON U., a university, but one with good student-faculty rapport and a sense of community.

WELLS, another good small women's college.

WESTERN MARYLAND, a place whose seniors shine in the Medical College Aptitude Test.

WHEATON (Mass.), another good women's-college-gone-coed that's a bargain for men.

WHITMAN, one of the best in the Pacific Northwest.

WILLAMETTE, another good one in the Northwest.

WITTENBERG, in Ohio, is a bargain for the middling student.

WOFFORD, a Southern school, heavily preprofessional, that has produced many scholars and leaders.

WORCESTER POLYTECHNIC, one of the good engineering schools; it has a curriculum that sees to it that engineers get an education.

The few state institutions listed above are there because they're primarily undergraduate like Miami, or are colleges like St. Mary's and William and Mary, or are clusters of small colleges like California's Santa Cruz and San Diego.

The Big State Universities

State universities that are particularly attractive to out-of-state students are:

California at Berkeley	Vermont
Colorado	Virginia
Michigan	Wisconsin
North Carolina	Texas
Penn State	

In the academic pecking order, giant Berkeley is at the top of the heap, but its fame is on the graduate level. An undergraduate pretty much has to be able to make it on his own, with little help from or contact with its famed faculty, and with perhaps a 50 percent chance of getting the classes he wants. The Riverside campus, with fifty-two hundred students, is a far more familial, supportive place and a well-kept secret that is likely to provide a much more fulfilling undergraduate experience.

Michigan and Wisconsin are two of the world's greatest universities, but 73 to 80 percent of the freshman and sophomore instruction is by teaching assistants; the scholars are occupied with being scholars, so the young customer is shortchanged. But nowhere are standards higher, and if one has excellent high school grades, the honors programs are without peer and offer more than most Ivy universities. Or one of the good small residential programs can give the benefits of a small-college learning community. Wisconsin probably has more diversity and more pizzazz than any public institution, which is consonant with its tradition of being, with Minnesota, the nation's most progressive state. Michigan is probably the most sophisticated, and given the limitations on out-of-state enrollment, has more diversity than anyone is going to be able to take advantage of.

Vermont is popular and selective because it's small—seven thousand students—and much clubbier than any other state university. Also, it's in Vermont, which means not only New England cachet but skiing and Lake Champlain.

Virginia, which has the architecturally most beautiful campus in the land, now has students almost to match. In the sixties it was a different story. Then, as an administrator at a college whose students were complaining that our tough curriculum was causing widespread brain-burnout, I asked deans at thirty institutions how many hours a week they believed their students studied. The answers ranged from well over forty hours at Haverford to the Virginia dean's "We have no idea; all we know is that we're producing more than the market can absorb and our only recourse is to flunk them out." But since then, an infusion of Yankee administrators and going coed has had a synergistic effect; a few of its departments in the humanities are now ranked among the best, while the admissions competition provided by the women has given it a very able student body. Virginia's honors program, however, is limited to a preselected group of freshmen who are relieved of course requirements and have independent study opportunities.

The universities of North Carolina, Texas, and Penn State are all prestige institutions but assembly lines for the undergraduates unless they're in honors programs. Texas, for example, has nearly fifty thousand students, as does Ohio State, which practices freshmanicide; because Ohio has to admit state high school graduates, it flunks them out at an appalling rate unless they have very large muscles and all-pro reflexes. And a former faculty member now at a good college said teaching at Penn State was like "pulling teeth."

Popular University of Colorado offers a beautiful setting, skiing, and a 60 percent attrition rate.

Alabama, Arkansas, Indiana, Iowa, Michigan State, Mississippi, South Carolina—and just about every state university—offer honors programs that provide stimulating intellectual havens for the serious students as well as contact with faculty members and most of the good qualities of the undergraduate college.

First-rate institutions in their technical fields, such as Purdue, Iowa State, Georgia Tech, Texas A&M, and the like in other states offer some of the world's finest vocational preparation in their areas, but the person who wants a good liberal education should examine any one of them with a cold appraising eye before plighting his troth. For example, Clemson's president resigned because the board of trustees wouldn't approve his cleaning up the school's athletic recruiting scandals. That sort of thing has to affect the atmosphere of a place (even if it doesn't have a football coach who, when penalized for unsportsmanlike conduct, was quoted in a Greenville, S.C. newspaper as saying, "I shouldn't of went out on the field.") Some of these primarily land-grant institutions, like Iowa State, Michigan State, and New Mexico State, are as much liberal arts as agriculture or engineering schools. In short, the watchword always is: Sample and test the merchandise.

On these lists there is at least one college that will meet the needs of almost any young person. It covers the spectrum. And the schools are the kind that will contribute to one's growth, which is what counts in the long run. It is not, as I noted in the beginning, intended to be, and could hardly be, encyclopedic. Since there are about ten times as many four-year institutions as I've mentioned, this was just intended to help in your search for the right kind of college for you. If it emboldened you to look at a strange school, that's good, because whether you or your friends have ever heard of it is completely irrelevant. Whether it will be a good lifetime match after your friends have long been forgotten is what counts.

11 ♫
While You're Still in High School

Some Commonsense Tips on Your Program and Activities

Every spring, several young clients who hope to go to fairly selective colleges will have planned senior-year schedules something like this:

> English   Computer Science
> Algebra II   Chemistry or Earth Science

They're often disturbed when I tell them they won't have a chance of getting into any of their ideal colleges, and almost invariably the reply is: "But that's all I need for graduation."

The trouble with this rationale is that an admissions director who can be selective has no interest in what the high school's minimum requirements are. He's looking for the best records in his pile of applicants, not the skimpiest. Thus, if a student is unwilling to carry a full load of at least four academically demanding, or "solid," courses all four years, his choice of colleges is going to be severely limited, and the ones he wants won't want him.

The program cited is minimal. Earth Science is easier than chemistry or physics, computer science is not an academic course, and Algebra II means the student will have three rather than four years of math. And there is no foreign language. In other words, it has only three academic "solids" (solids will be defined later), and one of those—Earth Science—is suspect as the easy way out.

The moral is that the tough row is the best one to hoe, for some good reasons:

First, high school is part of your education, not just a stepping-stone to college.

Second, taking easy courses will lower the admissions officer's estimation of you, no matter how good the grades. In a competitive situation this will disqualify you, no ifs, ands, or buts; period.

Third, taking the easy route is harmful to your moral fiber, and moral fiber is far more essential to your well-being than dietary fiber because it is something that will help determine what kind of person you become and what you accomplish in life.

A friend of mine says, "I got my education at Andover and I went to college at Yale." Whether or not he's exaggerating, he has a timely and relevant point because too many teenagers regard high school as something to be manipulated to the best advantage for college acceptance. Like writing an application essay for effect rather than for self-revelation, it will be counterproductive in the long run. (All this does not apply to those with special problems. They will be discussed later on.)

The first thing any good admissions director looks at is the quality of the program: does this student have four years each of English, math, science, and language, and has he carried at least four academic solids—preferably five—all four years? How many of them are honors or Advanced Placement courses? This tells him how significant the grades and class rank are because it reveals the quality of the goods. All Bs in an impressively tough program beats all As in an easy program any day of the week. That truth is worth belaboring; any sensible person would react that way and admissions officers are sensible people. Nor are they easily fooled.

To be in the competition for the very selective schools, it is absolutely necessary to have taken several of the top-ranked courses, whether they're honors or Advanced Placement, or if they're not available, the top level of a multiple track system. Without top quality courses, it is useless to apply to the most selective schools unless it is a most unusual case in which the applicant has some extraordinary talent or accomplishment to offer.

After sitting in an Amherst freshman English class a few years ago, I asked the professor if the kids could write—since I have a conviction that 95 percent of American high school students never get an adequate college-prep writing course (which I define as a theme a week for a full year). His reply was, "They've all had AP English, so it's just a matter of getting the garbage out in the first six weeks. After that they're all right." (By garbage, he meant the same thing a Deerfield School teacher is reputed to have said: "Men, read over your compositions, and when you come to a line you think is especially fine, strike it out!") In a math or a language or a science class they all would have had AP courses too.

Don't think that just because you have straight As in English in a good suburban high school you've proved your point. I find teachers in the best high schools in the Washington, D.C., and other suburbs miss more syntactical sins, sloppy rhetoric, awkward sentences, and appalling word usage than they catch. (My clients are asked to bring in two graded compositions, preferably expository.) Many a teacher has given As and Bs on papers that would get Ds or Fs in any respectable freshman comp course. One client with an SAT verbal of 300 had straight Bs in English at Bethesda–Chevy Chase High. The verbal score gauged his skills accurately. And this year I painfully had to explain to two conscientious girls that the themes their teachers had given them As on wouldn't pass muster at the colleges they were considering.

What Are Solids and What Are Semisolids?

The academically "solid" subjects are the college-prep courses in English, math, foreign languages, science, and social sciences. The normal sequence of ninth grade lab science, biology, chemistry, and physics, for example, are solid courses. So are the math courses from Algebra I through calculus.

Semisolids might be statistics instead of calculus, journalism, and one-semester courses in sociology, psychology, or religion. Taking a second year of biology instead of physics, or the easy chemistry course instead of the tough one with the equations, or earth science instead of physics is taking a semisolid route that won't work in a very competitive situation.

Computer science is learning how to use a machine; consumer math, shop, studio art, home economics–type courses, driver's or phys. ed, and typing aren't even counted by most colleges.

It's fine to have as many semisolid, or "fluffy," art, shop, or gourmet food courses as there's room for, on top of a *full* plate of the meat-and-potatoes courses.

What About Extracurricular Activities?

If a college can afford to be selective enough, it is going to demand some evidence of interests outside of studying; it would much prefer not to load up on grinds. The interest doesn't have to be a school activity, but it should be one in which the person has persisted and accomplished something. The late Bill Wilson of Amherst used to say, "I could take any ninth-grader with a butterfly collection and get him into any college in the country." By the time the kid was a senior, Bill would have had him a serious lepidopterist who would have been writing about his collecting or discovery expeditions.

If it's a school activity, the same rule of involvement and accomplishment applies. It hardly means a thing to list membership in the Spanish or French clubs, Key Club or Junior Achievers or whatever, unless one has been active and has an office or some achievement to show for it. Such joiner lists tend to be liabilities since they obviously are only for show.

Athletic ability in the minor sports opens the doors to a lot of good schools where no scholarships are involved. Good lacrosse, tennis, and golf players, for instance, can get into Lafayette or Hobart or Hopkins or Cornell when they wouldn't have otherwise. So can good actors, singers, oboe players, or debaters. One girl got into Bryn Mawr because she had a short story published. Princeton took one young friend because he won a national essay contest; until that time, Princeton had rated his chances at 30 percent. He now is a college philosophy professor. The key in such highly competitive places is outstanding accomplishment. In the case of the athlete or the actor, the college may have need of a particular skill; in the cases of the writers, they were giving evidence of promise that might reflect credit on the institution in the future.

Three of the best colleges in the Northeast and three elsewhere were eager to have this fellow, who was neither athlete, actor, nor big man on campus in his prep school. His only school activities were writing movie reviews for the school paper and organizing a film club. But in the seventh grade he had started writing a weekly movie review for his family, complete with news items and weekly quiz. He also had a formidable record and tape collection and two hundred pieces of musical equipment, all of which he had earned the money for. As an avid fan of the Minnesota Twins and their five-foot-seven-inch-tall star Kirby Puckett, he had also been working on a baseball simulation on the computer. It is important to note here that this interest came through on his personal statements and essays. For as he said, "Every time I don't review a movie, I feel I'm missing something." He needed to analyze his experience. One admissions director, after hearing about him, said, "Unless he's an ax murderer, I'll take him." But he went elsewhere, to Vassar, whose admissions director was no whit less enthusiastic.

What About Aptitude Testing?

Every year, nervous parents of high school seniors ask whether they shouldn't have their son or daughter take a battery of tests, either because the youngster isn't doing well in school or doesn't know what he or she wants to do. If there's a learning problem, it probably surfaced in the early grades; furthermore, most school systems have been testing the kids up one side and down the other for twelve years. If a teenager isn't doing well—and it's usually the male of the species—it may be garden variety adolescent rebellion, more than usual conflict with parents, or inability or unwillingness to compete with an achieving parent or sibling.

This "second-child syndrome" of not making an effort when the youngster is living in the shadow of a sibling or a parent is fairly common and it usually disappears when the affected child gets away and is accepted as his or her own person, not so-and-so's little (or big) brother or sister. In such cases it may be useful to consult a good psychologist or psychiatrist to be sure there isn't a personality difficulty or some learning problem that the school system hasn't discovered. But if that's not the case and it's a matter of not performing, mere aptitude testing isn't going to provide the blinding light on the road to Damascus. Hardly anybody knows enough about himself as a teenager to know what's going to engage him when he's a different, mature individual twenty years from now. A good college experience and life itself will provide plenty of aptitude testing in good time. Having a career goal is about as relevant to a good college experience as what kind of car the family has. Besides, just who knows how to program a sixteen-year-old?

It might make parents feel a little less test-driven to hear what Dr. James Powell, now president of Reed College, said when he was provost at Oberlin: "The kids who worry me are the ones who are so darn sure they know what they're going to be doing."

What About Going to College Early?

Going to college after the eleventh grade is a happy solution for a good student who is not being challenged but is just putting in time, frustrated and bored, intellectually and socially. But this doesn't happen often in the large, competitive suburban high schools. It's far more likely in very small schools with inadequate resources and where an interested student might not have anyone to talk to. The student should be mature enough socially to make the jump, be eager to do it, and know what she's getting into by making the kind of college visits discussed in that chapter. I say she because the cases I've had have nearly all been girls. All of the early college decisions were good moves for those particular students; for others they might have been disasters. One was a bright girl in a very small school who went to a good college at age sixteen, after the eleventh grade. A good freshman record enabled her to transfer to Wellesley, which had been her long-time ambition and might have been difficult to achieve from the secondary school she attended.

What About the Students with Special Problems?

Whatever the problem, the central consideration is the healthy development of the child. If the dyslexic student is making progress and can negotiate it, he should get out of the special program and into the school mainstream as soon as he can, simply because in college and in life that's where he's going to have to compete.

If he can take the college-prep courses, he should do so; if he can't, remember that there is a college for everyone, one where he can have a good experience. There are colleges where the math requirements, for instance, are minimal or non-existent; there are colleges with special, professional help for those who need it. Indeed, one dyslexic made it through two years of a demanding college that did not have any formal help program, simply because caring faculty members gave him oral exams and let him tape-record his papers. Then he transferred to a school that had agriculture courses.

Parents Should Be Fearlessly Militant About Teaching Quality.

There are more than enough mediocre high school teachers who keep their jobs because parents don't get nasty enough about the damage being done to their kids. They're often afraid of reprisals if they complain or take action. If the cause is just, it won't hurt the child if they complain; an attempt at reprisal would likely backfire. For, as mentioned elsewhere, a bad recommendation that didn't fit the pattern of the student's performance and whole record would be suspect.

Parents tend to run unduly scared. Kids who've been kicked out of elite prep schools on all manner of charges, from beer parties to drug selling, have been welcomed by first-rate colleges. One, who had been caught in a widely reported "drug bust" at an elite prep school, had no problem whatever and wound up in an Ivy school.

An object lesson for timid parents and students as well is that of a young friend at a private prep school who bucked the headmaster, no holds barred. He attacked the headmaster in the student newspaper as being untrue to his trust for not instituting an honor code the students had voted for. Nor did he rest with that; he wrote a formal complaint to the regional accrediting agency. This wave-maker who refused to take counsel of his fears was accepted at Amherst, Dartmouth, Duke, Georgetown, Michigan, Penn, and Williams.

In short, the easy way is just as wrong here as everywhere else.

12 🐟
Judging Yourself
as an Applicant

From Learning-Disabled to Valedictorian

In the anxious process of judging yourself as a college applicant, it might be comforting to know that a Harvard professor
has complained that today's admissions policies would have
excluded many of that institution's most illustrious alumni,
including presidents Franklin Roosevelt and John Kennedy.
Had he been a Yale prof he could have said the same thing
about many of its famous sons, including ambassador-
governor-presidential adviser W. Averell Harriman, who was a
C student there.

Furthermore, a famous scientist, Rita Levi-Montalcini, founder of Rome's Laboratory of Cell Biology, looking back on her
long life and those of her peers and colleagues, says that the
keys to personal success and fulfillment are not "the degree of
intelligence nor the ability to carry out one's tasks with thor-
oughness and precision." More important, she says, are total
dedication and a tendency to underestimate difficulties, "which
cause one to tackle problems that other, more critical and acute
persons instead opt to avoid."

There's nothing new about all this; Moses complained to the

Lord that he not only was a slow learner, he had a speech impediment—learning-disabled we'd call it today. George Washington wasn't famed as an intellectual, nor was Harry Truman. But all three of them did pretty well. It's just as I've been saying everywhere I could: motivation and desire fuel the bold, successful life. Or, as *Ecclesiastes* had it, "Again I saw that under the sun the race is not to the swift . . . nor riches to the intelligent . . . but time and chance happen to them all." And both time and chance tilt toward the one with dedication and desire.

Such dramatic stuff is folk knowledge to admissions people. As the late Bill Wilson of Amherst responded to a successful young man he had rejected ten years earlier, "I wish I had a nickel for every Pulitzer Prize winner I've turned down." And one of his famous colleagues, Alden Thresher of MIT, advocated choosing freshman classes by random selection, since all the applicants were qualified. The wise Mr. Thresher, however, didn't propose making admissions officers technologically obsolete until he'd retired. But in the college-going rush of the fifties, the president of Michigan State reportedly told his admissions office at one point to accept the next hundred applications that came in, no exceptions. The story is that this group did just as well as those selected by the wisdom of the admissions staff.

Random selection is still proposed every once in a while as the only fair way for the highly selective colleges to choose their freshman classes, and for very good reasons. While it is central to admissions mythology that the keepers of the gates are judging and rewarding individual merit, the track records of their picks show them to be poor handicappers. As evidence elsewhere in this book shows, there is a startling lack of correlation between selectivity and alumni achievement.

There are two solid reasons why the elite schools' gatekeepers don't and can't judge merit. One is that their real purpose is to admit the applicants they think can help the school achieve its own political, social, athletic, and status goals. And status is the most precious goal of all. Under truth serum almost any highly selective college director would admit he's afraid to have a high school counselor see him take anyone with a verbal score under 600. He'd be branded as willing to take the lesser students. Anyone who scores in the middle 400s on the verbal part of the SATs can do the work at any selective college, and study after study has underscored the common knowledge that there's no connection between college grades and later achievement—except for mathematicians, who are born and not made.

One of those studies, by psychologists at Harvard, Boston, and Wesleyan universities, found that the most outstanding students in college are the ones most likely to be unhappy ten years after graduation. And there was absolutely no correlation between scholastic achievement and later getting top jobs, high income, or similar accomplishments.

Another, by Dr. Douglas Heath of Haverford, whose long-term work on the effects of the college experience is cited in Chapter 9, went even further. He found that those with the best college records were less mature and less competent ten to fifteen years later than those of modest academic success. They tended to be more self-centered and had "tense and distant" relationships at work, and at home "less intimate relations with their wives." In short, the academic world is putting its highest valuations on the wrong people for the wrong reasons. They are ignoring character, the development of which, Dr. Heath says, should be central to the mission of liberal education. It follows then that by using academic statistics as the principal measures of worth the admissions people are not serving the public good.

The other reason is that no one has yet found an acceptable way to describe merit; much less, how to decide whether one ability or talent is better than another.

It is not unusual to hear admissions officers say that most of the personal statements they read are boring, dull, or wimpishly playing it safe. That's the kind of answer I usually get when I ask about the quality of their applicants' essays. The Yale admissions director has been quoted as saying they're all bland. So why was Yale admitting them; what good for the individual or for the virility of a nation was its selection process accomplishing? Are the admissions staffs serving a democratic society well? They're playing it safe, protecting themselves. The whole situation calls to mind a successful author's efforts to warn a would-be freelance writer about another group that plays it safe: "Every editor ought to be horsewhipped every day in the public square."

So, the message is that if you're turned down by a very selective school, consider the source; it's not a verdict on your quality, your ability, or your prospects in life, no matter how much it hurts the ego. It means only that you're not getting into that academic club. But take heart, equally good schools are looking for you, schools you someday may be urging your own kids to consider.

If You're Learning-Disabled

A learning disability does not bar success in college. On the contrary, it may contribute to success in college and after. The dyslexic and the problem learner of some other kind, having had to work to conquer or compensate for some handicap or disability, usually has more motivation to succeed, and that's 95 percent of the battle almost anywhere.

Several years ago I had a client who'd graduated from a New England prep school in spite of a bad case of dyslexia that had not been discovered—unbelievable as that seems—until he was in the eleventh grade. He worked hard at a compensatory program and graduated from a very good college. Another, whose disability was such that, from the age of twelve to fifteen, he'd been in an exceedingly costly private school for dyslexics, insisted on getting into the public school mainstream as a junior because "in the special school people weren't working." By his senior year he was getting As and Bs in a fairly competitive suburban high school. His highest SAT verbal score was 370.

But his math was an unusual 700. At this writing he is a junior at St. Andrews College with a 3.7 average. He hopes to go to Georgia Tech next year for the engineering part of the 3–2 program that many liberal arts colleges have with engineering schools.

In a quarter century I have seen kids with every kind of disability you can think of—brain damage from leukemia therapy, blindness, and the many manifestations of dyslexia—go to college and prosper. But whatever the problem, they had one thing in common: they worked at it, and thereby overcame or compensated for it.

My most dramatic case was one that sparkles with the extra-thyroid energy and determination Emerson had in mind when he wrote: "What will you have, quoth God. Pay for it and take it." In the winter of 1988 this young man was a senior at American University getting mostly Cs and a few Bs, besides running a very successful home construction business. But four years ago, he started his college application essay in these exact words: "Dyslexia is a problem which has hoovered [sic] over me for the entirety of my life."

When he started working with a tutor in the seventh grade, he said, "I would read something and not understand a word of it. . . . I would have to read every word with a teacher. Even then I might not understand a word of it. . . . I would review the material until I reached a point of exhaustion. . . . By my sophomore year, however, I was doing the initial work myself with only guidance and correction from others. At present I am able to independently read a work such as *Hamlet*, comprehend the plot, and respond to questions. Skills at this level have made it possible for me to maintain a C+ average in a college prep school despite my learning disability." Those skills were the fruit of dogged effort. He said he spent ten hours on his *Hamlet* report, but he wrote it without any help. His SAT verbal went from 370 in 1983 to 470 in 1984.

If you think he harbored any self-doubts, consider this: he applied to eighteen colleges, six of which were Grade A schools

I had talked to about him. He got acceptances from sixteen, was wait-listed at one, and rejected by only one! Of course, admissions officers were sure he would pay the price.

Another fellow whose eyesight was so poor that he had been judged legally blind made much use of tapes and talking books. In the tenth grade he decided he wanted to go to college, worked harder, raised his grades from Cs and Ds to Bs and Cs and his verbal score rose one hundred points. He did well enough in college that he won a graduate fellowship to Carnegie-Mellon. Another example is that of a girl, blind from birth, who won honors in French at the University of Rochester.

If You're in the Great Middle Range

The problem for the overwhelming majority of high school seniors is not so much the worry about getting in as it is in making an intelligent choice. Most of the good—but not necessarily well-known—colleges don't have the problem of turning down two to six persons for every one they admit. Nevertheless, they want a respectable performance in a solid college-prep program that includes at least three years each of math, science, and language, and an SAT verbal of 500, maybe less. And don't be intimidated by what a directory lists as a college's range of scores; the chances of its being accurate are not great, and its chances of applying to your particular case are probably very small. You can get a clue by consulting a directory that shows whether the school takes 60, 70, or 80 percent of its applicants, or only 50.

The lower the percentage of applicants a college accepts, the greater the competition, since the law of supply and demand is in control. If the percentage is 50, you're likely to need a strong B to B+ average. If it's 80 percent, it may take only a strong C average (and the 80 percent school may be the better one). Because a school's applicant pool varies in size and quality from year to year, it's hard to be much more specific.

If the acceptance percentage is low, you'll need evidence of continued, active interest and achievement in some activity outside of class to be competitive. Just a list of club memberships is meaningless; it's a fake front. And even if there's been some activity in one of them, remember that quality, not quantity, is what counts. Your activity doesn't have to be a school-related one.

The lower the grades and scores, the better and more persuasive the personal statement and essay, as well as outside interests, have to be. As one admissions director said of a prospect with marginal statistics, "He'd better knock our socks off with his personal statement." Sometimes a convincing statement for wanting to go to a particular college helps, but it has to have a rationale; just gushing won't do.

If You're Interested in a Nontraditional College

A school that is out of the usual mold, such as Hampshire, will want to make sure that you will fit in. Compatibility, not competition, is the controlling factor. Highly intellectual and demanding places like Deep Springs, New College, Reed, and St. John's are not competitive. In some recent years not all have filled their freshman classes. But they are carefully selective. Such colleges, even if they have barely enough bodies to fill the class, won't accept a candidate they think won't fit in and prosper. And that decision has more to do with the kind of person one is than grades or scores. These colleges, like Evergreen, Bennington, Marlboro, Goddard, tiny Thomas Aquinas in California, or Antioch, are not places where most high school seniors can stand the freedom or the intellectual emphasis or the small size of the community.

In short, anyone thinking of a nontraditional college had better do an earnest job with the chapter on self-examination, because the consequences, as previously noted, will be either deep satisfaction or acute dissatisfaction.

Judging Yourself for Ivy-type Competition

Straight A averages and 1400 or 1500 or even 1600 on the college boards aren't enough. Students and parents both often think they can get in anywhere with such figures. 'Tain't so. As mentioned elsewhere, some very selective places like Duke turn down over one third of all the valedictorians who apply. Unless it's a tiny high school, class rank is one of the three critical statistical criteria, along with grades and scores. But it's a waste of effort to apply if good statistics are all you have to offer.

What it takes to be in the competition is not only excellent grades—say at least a 3.5 average for openers—but several Advanced Placement and honors courses and a solid program of four years each of math, science, and foreign language, in addition to English and the social sciences. And the transcript should show five academic solids each year. In the demanding new magnet high schools of science and technology (modeled after the Bronx High School of Science) springing up here and there around the country, every student takes seven solids a semester and thus gets even more science and math. For this demanding regimen, at least three to four hours of study a day are needed, compared to one or two for most of his suburban peers. As more such schools come into being, the competition is going to get still tougher. And if it isn't already crystal clear, the teenager who has gotten all As in an easy program has wasted educational opportunities as well as his time. He's cast into the outer darkness.

Just as important as top grades in a demanding program and good test scores are persistence and success in an outside interest or interests. Both words—persistence and success—are important. Not only do the very selective colleges shun grinds, but a seven-year study by the Educational Testing Service involving twenty-five thousand applicants and nine colleges found sticking with an outside interest and accomplishing something in it was a strong predictor of academic, leadership, and social accomplishments in college.

The activity or interest can be almost anything. But the achievement has to be not just substantial but outstanding, such as winning a national essay contest, a regional scholastic, forensics, or debate competition, being chosen for the all-state band, or being the person the high school administration turns to for the most responsible student roles.

In athletics it is what the high school coach has to say to his college counterpart that opens the door. Achievement in some field less crowded than athletics or music can often be a greater asset. You'll stand out if you are the only applicant who has spent four years building an active Temple youth group, as its president staged a two-way television exchange program with a similar group in Moscow, and been a statewide leader to boot. You'll be one of a kind, whereas the fullback has to compete with a lot of other first-rate athletes for the one fullback slot.

Naturally, the personal statement and essay parts of the application have to show a good brain at work and good thoughts skillfully expressed. Writing that would pass muster other places won't do when you're competing with some of the brightest teenagers in the land. In this kind of competition a slapdash or poorly done personal statement or essay can hang an otherwise four-star applicant. See the next chapter, A Good Application = Open Sesame.

Whoever You Are

If you've had or have a learning problem, don't give up on yourself; there's at least one college—and probably five or six—where you can have a successful experience that will contribute to your development. In my experience at least, I have never seen a hopeless case, although some have come to me thinking theirs was hopeless.

If you're in the Great Middle of the C and B students, don't underestimate yourself. Try to get into the toughest college you can that seems compatible with your goals and values.

If you march to a different drummer, do your self-examination with great care and candor.

If you're seeking an Ivy school, don't overestimate your credentials. It's difficult to realize how many hundreds, or thousands, have as good or better. In 1988, over eighty-three thousand had verbal scores of 600 or better and over ten thousand had scores of 700 or over. And most of them were applying to the same group of colleges.

A final caution: Don't think that the name of your suburban high school carries any special magic that will let you in. It's what you've done. Just about everybody you're in competition with goes to a good competitive suburban high school with a lot of bright kids. The only exceptions would be some of the Bronx High School of Science clones or a handful of the most demanding prep schools.

Whoever you are, remember that it's not an admissions committee that makes the real judgment on you; it will only be you.

13

A Good Application = Open Sesame

A Statement That Reveals Who You Are Can Often Work Wonders.

Believe it or not, a C student, and sometimes a D student, can write as effective an application as a valedictorian, often a better one. How so? Because the honest, self-revealing one is persuasive; sometimes it can even win an acceptance over better SAT scores and grades. But the cute, smart, affected, or phony one gags the bored reader and tilts that folder toward the reject pile.

You don't have to be a talented writer but you have to know your subject: yourself; you should feel strongly about what you're saying, whether the topic is frivolous or serious, and you must say it sensibly and grammatically. Also, it is absolutely crucial to write for an audience of one: yourself. Then it will have the eloquence of honesty. But if it's written with an eye to "what do they want?" you're dead. "They" want to know who you are, and you'll never be able to tell them if you're looking at them instead of yourself. All you'll do is defeat your purpose and turn off the reader.

Unless it's something that's been simmering on the back burner of your mind for some time and just comes to a boil, you're probably going to have to redo it a couple of times at least to make it say what you want it to say. Every professional writer has to rewrite and rewrite; so why should you expect to get it right the first time? The human brain works slowly; as *The New Yorker*'s famed James Thurber explained, "I'm not a writer; I'm a rewriter." A very good high school debater, now a Harvard alumnus, rewrote his statement three times before he was telling why he debated, rather than what he had achieved, which was already in the data part of his application.

The whole purpose of the essays is to provide a glimpse of you as a person, to give insight that the objective data do not. That glimpse gets points for being well thought out and well written, and gets marked down for being sloppily handled. The assigned topics test your imagination, thinking, and writing ability. These two personal parts give you the chance to set yourself apart from the rest of that great pile of folders, to make your application come alive. When you're in a competitive situation, at least half of those thousands of folders will have as good or better statistics and credentials, whether you want to think so or not. That means that what you say about yourself is crucial. The interview is nothing by comparison—in fact, many of the most competitive places would like to eliminate them, or they pay them little mind. When you've performed below your ability, or for some other reason consider yourself a late bloomer, what you say about yourself can save you or hang you.

On the personal statement essay (the question that asks you to tell something about yourself that you want the college to know), imagine you're responding to a pen pal from another land or civilization wanting to know what makes you tick, what's important to you, how you live. There are no holds barred; as Horton the elephant said in Dr. Seuss's book *Horton Hatches an Egg*, "I say what I mean and I mean what I say." No matter

how far out the topic or viewpoint, if it's genuine and supported it will be effective, even when it flaunts the arro-
gance of youth. When Bennington College was at its peak of
selectivity a good many years back, a client was asking me
what she should say in her application, for, she explained,
"I really don't know what college can teach me." I said, "If
that's what you really believe, say so and say why." The
next time I had occasion to call Bennington, an incredulous
admissions director asked me, "Do you know what that
G——— girl said in her application?" Bennington accepted
her.

Two Important Things to Do Before Starting an Essay

1. Do the self-examination suggested in Chapter 3. That will
get your thinking on track and very likely suggest a topic.

2. Read the second and the last chapters of *The Elements
of Style* by Strunk and White. This magic little book is the best
thing ever written on how to use your mother tongue effectively.
The principles in those thirty-seven small pages are worth more
than everything else that's ever been or is now being written
on the subject of college application essays. They will put up
road signs for you; they will keep you out of the ditch, and
prevent you from crossing the double yellow lines.

How Long Does It Have to Be?

Just long enough to make your point, and no longer. If the
instructions say to keep it within a certain space, do so; otherwise; try to do it in two hundred words; it will be more
effective than if you take four hundred. There's a hoary news-
paperman's saying that goes: "I didn't have time to write a short
story." The long one is the verbose, easily written one. See the
two gems under "Assigned Topic."

One Central Thing to Keep in Mind While Writing

Use the whats to hang the whys onto. And be specific about them; give the details. A general statement not supported is bad writing. Only damage is done by writing such things as "My trip exposed me to other cultures" or "I learned the value of hard work from my victory." You may think these are true and profound, but your reader will only gag. You don't have to beat your breast; the data have already recorded your feats or failures. This is where you explain why you did it, or why it meant something to you, or what it did for you, or why you sinned, and whether and why you've changed. When you do this, you're giving the reader a feeling for you as a human being, which is what he wants.

After You've Written a Draft

Read it aloud to see how it sounds; if it sounds queer or stiff, it is.

Rework it and ask a friend to read it. An unbiased opinion is valuable, and a friend is better for this usually than a parent, who tends to be too emotionally involved in the project, and often much too cautious, as we will see further on.

There Are No Bad Topics, But—

There are only bad ways of handling topics. You can avoid emptiness, pretension, cuteness (clever is fine *if* it's the real thing), and other sins by writing honestly and imaginatively about something important to you, no matter how trivial. But it has to be something that only you could write, because you're telling, in specific detail, what it did to you. Generalizations that anyone could write are not just useless, they're boring.

Don't write about your trip unless you have something more specific and less pretentious to say than "I have had the thrilling adventure of exploring a variety of landscapes from the tumultuous terrain of Alaska to the mystic fiords of Norway. . . . Travel . . . has deepened perception, broadened imagination, sharpened sensitivity, and refined the intellect." As Jeannette Hersey, former Connecticut College admissions director, said of personal essays, "Ninety-five percent of them are travelogues." They tell where the person has been or what he or she has done, but not why he or she did it or precisely what he or she got from it.

Here are excerpts from one that Jeannette Hersey or anyone else would rank high in the good 5 percent because this travel obviously did do something to the intellect:

> The first few years of my life were spent in the suburbs of Washington, D.C., where I attended a small private boys' school. I was no more concerned with my future then than any young American kid whose main interests were in collecting baseball cards and chasing the Good Humor man. . . . My life dramatically changed, however, when my family moved to Yarmouth, Nova Scotia. . . . Suddenly, I was thrust from a suburban American lifestyle to that of a rural Canadian town of 8,000. At the outset I was shocked, but gradually I began to understand and appreciate the differences between Yarmouth and Washington. . . . I have never met as many generous, caring, and trusting people. . . . Even something as simple as yielding right-of-way to pedestrians at an intersection is a reflection of the unhurried lifestyle that allows time for the consideration of others. The smallness of the town causes everyone to know everyone, and thus engenders a trust for others. It is, therefore, not unusual to find a clothing store manager who would sell you a pair of pants even if you were a few dollars short, knowing you would pay him later. . . . This . . . lifestyle was very secure . . . and even for those who left it, the town became a retreat from the outside world they often found difficult to adjust to. . . . Most were never motivated to achieve a higher socio-economic status than the previous generation because it often required leaving the "nest." The end result for some were lives that revolved around a six-foot slab of sidewalk in front of the Main Street pharmacy. . . . "Why should I work hard in school? My dad and brothers have never gone anywhere in life?" asked one of my closest friends

whose father was an alcoholic fisherman. I could sympathize with his lack of motivation and differing goals, but it was hard for me to accept his failing in school and thus I spent many tutorial hours helping him make the grade. . . . However, it would be a mistake to criticize the whole town as being without motivation. Their priorities were merely different, and success in many cases was not measured on an individual basis. . . . There was no greater disappointment than having rain on the day of a community picnic that had been planned for over a month. Nor for me was there any greater pleasure than witnessing the smile on an old canoe craftsman's face after his donated canoe was raffled off in support of the local fire department. In reflecting on my experience, I was often forced to ask the perplexing question, "What is success?" It had always seemed reasonable to equate success with happiness or peace of mind. . . . This revelation forced me to conclude that their priorities were simply different, but not worse than mine.

That piece give the reader a vivid picture of the writer, and Georgetown, Kenyon, Dension, and Dickinson thought so too.

Other favorite topics that are deadly without some message: Cutesy lists of things the essayist likes are hackneyed topics that arouse reader hostility, as do stories of successes, athletic or other; the death of a pet; autobiographies ("My name is . . . " or "Hello, I'm . . . "); statements of one's sterling qualities; and pontifications on one of the world's pressing issues.

In this account of one small athletic success, the writer makes an illuminating point about himself. He shows you—just as *The Elements of Style* says to—how winning one tennis match made him see how he was falling short. See how much more enlightening and engaging it is than some musty generality like, "Through winning I learned the virtue of self-discipline."

In my first tournament, during the summer of 1979, I really didn't strive to win and play to the best of my ability. My feeling was that

I'd be content with losing to a player of higher caliber than I was. My goal was not to lose to an opponent of less ability than mine. If I did lose to a person ranked below me, my personal ranking would be in jeopardy. The next year, halfway into the same tournament, I realized I had a chance to win the championship. I had beaten an opponent in the quarterfinals who was ranked above me and the rest of the players were no better than I was. This was when I realized how inappropriate my goal had been. From that point on I knew that if I wanted to win, I couldn't be content with losing; a ten-dollar entrance fee was paid to win, not to be satisfied with losing. That kind of expectation would not allow me to reach my expectations in tennis or in life. The result was that I went clear to the finals. I lost, and for the first time, I felt discouraged after losing to a player of a higher caliber. I wasn't satisfied in the manner in which I had approached the tournament. With better preparation and more confidence in myself, I could have won the match. Never again would I be content with losing. From then on, my goal was to win, nothing less. My practicing became more strenuous and my concentration level rose to a new high. I learned to discipline myself while practicing. By taking full advantage of my abilities, my Maryland state ranking rose from number 26 in 1980 to number 8 in 1981. This competitive spirit also applied to other aspects of my life. I was more motivated to complete my school work and to participate more actively in extra curricular activities. Instead of being trite and unappealing, school work became a challenge. . . .

He was accepted at Rensselaer, Worcester Polytechnic, University of Rochester, and Washington University, and is now a Defense Department engineer on a project in Bangkok.

A similarly effective vignette was written by the editor of a high school literary magazine, but his topic was people rather than prose because he found that:

. . . after four months on the job I consider the honor to be less important than the actual experience . . . a valuable opportunity to deal with human nature. . . . Differences of opinion and personality caused my job to take a turn I had not expected. Section editors and their assistants became enemies. . . . Business managers complained of interference. . . . I took the sensitive approach to the problem. I began a campaign of asking, not telling, people to try and work together. . . . This, and several individual conferences, has resulted in a more comfortable situation for everyone. . . . There is a great difference between this experience and, for example, my experiences on athletic teams. In crew there is one leader, the coxswain, who asks for no opinions. . . . As an editor I have found it is necessary to ask opinions, to accept advice and to be sensitive. . . . Life is not as simple as a narrow boat concerned only with speeding in a single direction. It is more like an organization of many individuals with multiple directions and speeds, all of which must be considered in the administration of leadership.

The admissions people at Vassar were won over by this perceptive piece of self-awareness.

In Search of a Topic

This comes close to being the universal agony, but it can be solved sooner or later, as one girl found, by asking yourself enough questions and thinking about what's interesting or important to you. The following example is an ideal model because the writer picked a subject important to her and then proved her point with specific examples of how music helped her in many different kinds of situations. The Caramellos provide a happy light touch:

After trying to write this essay for several weeks, I realized that I'm having trouble because I express my deepest feelings, not through words, but through music. Whenever I'm upset, or bored, or frustrated, or happy, I play the piano or listen to music. When I'm feeling happy I go to the piano and bang out "Magnetic Rag" by Scott Joplin or Debussy's second "Arabesque." When I'm tired or depressed I play through some Chopin Nocturnes or Joplin's "Bethena." When a friend of mine unexpectedly killed himself last spring and I had to spend several hours home alone just after hearing the news, I pounded into the piano Mozart's Sonata in A minor, which he wrote about the death of his mother. Somehow it helped. Later that spring, when I got an "A" on my English term paper, I came home, turned volume up to ten, and danced around to Bruce Springsteen. When I miss my friends from music camp, I listen to "Spring" from Vivaldi's *The Four Seasons*, which a close friend played in several recitals. I also listen to Moussorgsky's *Pictures at an Exhibition*, which the camp orchestra performed at its last concert. My mother once said that music is my emotional crutch. She could add chocolate and orange juice to that list. As I wandered around my house, looking for inspiration for this essay, I passed the boxes of chocolate bars that I'm selling to raise money for my school choir and barely resisted the temptation to demolish the Caramellos, thereby putting myself further in debt to the choir. I think I rely more on music than chocolate, however. At least it's not fattening. I started playing the piano when I was seven years old. I was eager to start because I had heard my mother and older sister playing for years. In fifth grade, my class staged *The Phantom Tollbooth* and I, after setting new words to the song "Tomorrow," played while my friends sang. Three years later I found myself once again at the piano while my friends sang as I accompanied my junior high school choir. The next year I practiced my scales in a damp little cabin in the middle of Maine during my first summer at New England Music Camp. Every morning at camp I watched the mist rise from the lake revealing white cottages surrounded by pines on the far shore. My days were filled with lessons, practice, and sports. I learned how to conduct; I learned how to sail; I learned how to clean toilets. And I concentrated on my music. Last summer I learned Beethoven's *Pathetique Sonata*. My favorite part about camp, however, was the people. They shared my love for music. I know this love will stay with me, whatever I do in life, to express my greatest joys and soothe my deepest disappointments.

Yale was lucky enough to get her, although others tried.

The Assigned Topic

Here the applicant had six inches of space in which to tell something about herself. She gave a one-two-three recitation of her interests and then hit a home run with her socko climax on her goals:

> My interests are varied. I like to draw, act, and ride. Most of my extracurricular activities involve drawing or acting. I am art editor of the literary magazine and of the yearbook, and I have played the leads in several plays, including *Taming of the Shrew*—but I have also managed the football and wrestling teams, and I am the movie critic for our two school newspapers. Last year I went to the Sidwell Friends School in Washington, D.C. on a school exchange program, and then I stayed over the summer in Virginia and worked as a riding teacher. Right now I am experimenting with myself; I am trying to find something I want to pursue in college and as a career. My problem, however, is that I like doing everything I have done. I love to draw; sometimes I want to be a famous artist and hang my paintings in the Metropolitan. But I also love to act, and sometimes I want to be a famous actress on Broadway. Sometimes I want to be president of IBM or of the United States. I want to be another Picasso, or Plato; I want to solve the world's peace problem and then discover the cure for cancer. My future plans are indefinite, but my goals are infinite. I want to do everything and be everything, and I want to be the best.

Facts that might be in the data part here illustrate the range of interests that tugged at her. From Johns Hopkins she went to Columbia as a Nicholson Fellow, working for a doctorate in English literature. A too-helpful parent might have tried to get her to cut the last sentence.

Here is another that makes its point on one page, in about three hundred words. The question was to describe some idea or intellectual experience that had an impact:

> My encounter with the mathematical limit changed my life by expanding my narrow views. Before exposure to it, I viewed the world in extremes; black and white, or good and evil. When a limit was first explained to me, I was mystified; how could a number be found to render an infinite expression finite? In other subjects, such

as English, I had learned that paradoxes existed; Charles Dickens wrote, "It was the best of times, it was the worst of times," but to me these were not insights into life, they were puzzles to tantalize the imagination and confuse the mind. The fact that mathematics, the field that I could always rely on to be logical, contained a paradox utterly confused me; yet this paradox eventually led to a deeper understanding of life. When, after many months of mental turmoil, my mind expanded to encompass this challenging idea, I began to view the world differently. If a numerical expression need not be finite or infinite, then why must an answer be correct or incorrect? Why must an action be good or bad? Why must people be intelligent or stupid? If parameters as strict as those bounding finite and the infinite can be bent, ignored, and at times surpassed, then how can terms as ambiguous as good, correct, and intelligent be strictly defined? Once this theory crystallized in my mind, I realized I had to change my perspective on life. As John Keats states so lyrically, life is not absolute; it is a glorious array of shades and intensities of all colors. Through my exposure to the conceptual limit, a new world was opened to me, a world without theoretical limit.

Amherst, whose question that was, got her. The disappointed suitors were Williams, Carleton, and Middlebury. Williams even offered her extra-early acceptance, although she hadn't even applied for early acceptance, and the Amherst admissions director wrote that she enjoyed reading the application. Who wouldn't?

Parental Help: The Great Peril

If an admissions officer suspects a student's statement is not his own work the almost certain reaction is rejection. I know of one case when an A student suffered such a fate. But short of that, parents often hurt by pressuring the youth to play it safe, to avoid mention of a sticky or controversial topic, or they try to impose their ideas of how a topic should be handled. One father, for example, didn't want his daughter to mention her work for the legalization of marijuana, although it fit in with her pattern of activism, not her habits. When she asked me, I told her to include it and say why. If the college had objected it wouldn't have been worth going to. Pointing out bad grammar or unsupported themes is all to the good; in short, the parent should only function as an eagle-eyed critic, not as creator or co-author. But no amount of warning is going to keep them from thinking that they can improve things, when what they usually do is censor all the spontaneity and life out of the essay.

Here is a dramatically convincing example of parental mal-feasance. The parent in this case, a Ph.D., is a full professor at a major university. He magnanimously consented to being an object lesson for other parents. His editing and corrections did not improve the quality or the impact of the daughter's essay, but his deletions robbed it of its life-giving touches of detail and of its endearing charm, such as the shared tastes of student and teacher in chewing gum, the dog's saliva on the wrapper, or her first visit to the art museum with her teacher.

The first version is how the father would have had it:

As I squeezed some yellow paint from the tube, I was reminded of the first time I used yellow acrylic paint or any acrylic paint for that matter . . . (3 or 4 lines) [space, he means]. All my life I had a fear of art. Although I enjoyed looking at the works of others, the thought of doing art myself made me uneasy. Expressing myself with paints and clay seemed strange and difficult. I dreaded work-ing on the first assignment in my Humanities class when I found out that it was to create an original poster. I had been in the art room many times before to look at my best friend, Mo's, paintings and drawings. She was in the advanced program and had her own studio across the hall. She was phenomenal. Her portraits of old people actually made me feel old. Before I knew it Mo had collected all the paints I needed for my poster. I sat there for what seemed like an hour staring at my poster board while Mo and everyone else seemed to be creating masterpieces. Finally I took a small amount of yellow paint on my brush, diluted it with water, and began to paint. I immediately deplored what I had done. I was ready to give up when I heard a voice behind me. It was the art teacher, Mr. Valimaki. Everyone called him "Mr. V." "Not bad" he said. I suddenly became embarrassed because I realized he was talking to me. "Oh no!" I said. "This is awful. I'm just not cut out for . . ." Mr. V. interrupted me. "These kind of look like building forms. Mind if I . . ." He smiled as he took the paint brush. I watched as he effortlessly made a few windows, fire escapes, and some lines. A city scene was emerging. He handed the paint brush back to me. "Keep going." I could hear him whistling down the hall. I added a few more lines.

I found myself in the art room more and more. The atmosphere was warm and welcoming. The room was wonderfully messy and lived in. I admired those students like Mo who had their own individual studios. They were all very experienced artists, but Mr. V treated everyone the same and saw potential in everyone. Whenever I got stuck, Mr. V would encourage me. He was honest and didn't hesitate to say that something was not as good as it could be. I was amazed that he remembered what all of his students were working on and the problems we were encountering. He trusted students and created an atmosphere that allowed us to be free with art. An atmosphere where we felt unhibited [sic] to try new things. He was an artist with a special love of art that enabled him to teach from within.

Mo and I decided that we would like to share the available studio work area the following year. We turned in our portfolios and hoped that we would get chosen to get one. We did. We got it. I was very eager to start another year of working with Mr. V. That summer Mr. V called me to tell me he got a job at an art career center. I was happy for him, but at the same extremely disappointed and somewhat hurt.

At the beginning of the year I lost interest in art. I felt I couldn't do it without Mr. V's help and encouragement. I became extremely jealous of Mo's talent in art. This bothered me because friends should be happy, not envious of each other. I thought I didn't deserve to be in advanced art and the only reason I was chosen was because Mr. V didn't want to hurt my feelings.

I went to visit Mr. V at his new school of all artists. I realized then that he had moved on and it was time for me to do the same. It was time to work on my own.

I was jolted from my thoughts by Mo's voice imitating Mr. V's "Not bad." She said I smiled as I felt my paint brush glide across the canvas.

This is the way the daughter wrote it:

As I squeezed some yellow paint from the tube, I was reminded of the first time I used yellow acrylic paint or any acrylic paint for that matter. . . .

All my life I had had a fear of art, not a fear of looking at it, but of doing it. I enjoyed going to museums, although I knew that I failed to appreciate a lot of the works, especially the more abstract pieces. The thought of doing art myself made me uneasy. Expressing myself with paints and clay seemed strange and difficult.

I dreaded the first assignment in my Humanities class when I found out it was to make an original poster expressing ideas about the arts. I had been in the art room many times to look at my best friend, Mo's art. She was in the advanced program and had her own studio across the hall. She was a phenomenal artist. Some of her portraits of old people actually made me feel old. Before I knew it Mo had gotten all the paints that I needed for my poster. I sat there for what seemed like an hour staring at my white poster board while Mo and everyone else seemed to be creating masterpieces. Finally I took a small amount of yellow paint, diluted it with water, and began to paint a design. I immediately deplored what I had done and was ready to give up when I heard a voice behind me. It was the art teacher, Mr. Valimaki. Everyone called him "Mr. V" for short. "Not bad" he said. I suddenly became embarrassed because I realized he was talking to me. "Oh no!" I said. "This is awful. I'm just not cut out for . . ." Mr. V interrupted me. "These kind of look like building forms." He smiled as he took the paint brush from my grasp. "Mind if I . . . ?" "No, no, go right ahead." I watched as he spontaneously made a few windows, fire escapes and some lines here and there. He handed the paint brush back to me. "Keep going," he said as he walked away. I could hear him whistle down the hall. I liked what he had done and realized that with some practice I could do it too. I added a few more lines.

I found myself in the art room more and more. The atmosphere was so warm and welcoming. The room was wonderfully messy and lived in. I really admired the students like Mo who had their own studio. They were all wonderful artists, but Mr. V treated everyone the same and saw potential in every person. Whenever I got stuck, Mr. V would encourage me. He was honest and didn't hesitate to say that something was not as good as it could be. It was amazing that he knew what every student was working on and the problems they were encountering. He trusted students and created an atmosphere that allowed one to be free with art. An atmosphere where we felt unhibited [sic] to try new things. He was an artist with a special love of art that enabled him to teach from within.

The first time I went to the museum with Mr. V. was like putting on a new set of glasses that allowed me to see form, shape, and feeling in the works that I had never realized before.

I began to stay after school to do art and just talk with Mr. V. We had so much in common from liking Trident spearmint gum and not minding having his dog Nevelson's saliva on the wrapper to James Taylor music. We laughed at the same things. He would tease me for being absent minded while searching for his keys for the 100th time. Sometimes we'd take breaks to plant flowers or feed the birds out in the courtyard.

Mo and I decided to apply for an art studio together for the following year. We got it. I was so excited for another year of working with Mr. V. That summer Mr. V. called me to tell me he got a job at an art career center. I was happy for him, but at the same time extremely disappointed and somewhat hurt.

At the beginning of the year I lost interest in art. I felt I couldn't do it without Mr. V's help and encouragement. I became extremely jealous of Mo's talent in art. This bothered me because friends should be happy, not envious of each other. I thought I didn't deserve to be in advanced art and the only reason I was chosen was because Mr. V didn't want to hurt my feelings.

I went to visit Mr. V at his new school of all artists. I realized then that he had moved on and it was time for me to do the same. It was time for me to work on my own.

I was jolted from my thoughts by Mo's voice imitating Mr. V's "Not bad." She said I smiled as I felt my paint brush glide across the canvas.

This girl was accepted at all seven very selective schools she applied to, won a $3,000 competition at one, and one dean told me he "loved" her essay.

The Very Personal Statement of the Underachiever or Child of Divorce

The person who hasn't performed anywhere near his ability has a chance to shrive himself when an application form asks, "What else would you like the admissions office to consider?" Or, he can append a statement telling why he hasn't done as well as he should. Divorce, for example, invariably affects a youth's performance if the breakup occurs around the age of puberty, and admissions officers are sensitive to this. Here is how one young man's honest confrontation with himself made believers of every admissions director who read it:

What else would you like the Admissions Office to consider in evaluating your application? Perhaps there is *personal information that would help in interpreting your academic record* or in *understanding you as an individual.* Transfer students should use this space to explain why you wish to attend William and Mary.

Boarding the plane I smiled, seeing that I was doing the right thing; but I wasn't. I was running away from my problems as I always had.

My family had forced me to run to England to go to school. Problems at home were too great for me to handle and any attempt to put the pieces back together would be futile. I had tried ever so hard and my school report had shown my emotional beating. My grades had plummeted and I did not even try to pick them up for I "had better things to do" even though I never found out what they were. The only thing I picked up was a shell to crawl into.

The day I arrived in England was dark and rainy; I wondered what had happened to my bright and cheery sanctuary. That day was a harbinger for the ones to come. Only part way through the year all my problems seemed to catch up with me and new ones constantly developed. I struggled through the longest year and left as soon as I could, right after the final exams. England's fertile land did not help me grow. I ran back to America and into a prep school.

On registration day everyone greeted me with a saccharine smile and gave me a handshake filled with insincerity, but the sky was blue and the day was pleasant. I put my room together, and dusted my top most shelf, and then only had four hours until dinner. That day I found out exactly how long four hours is. No year had been so painful; my grades stayed where they were, in mediocrity, no matter how hard I thought I worked; friendship seemed ever so scarce, and life seemed so fruitless. But, I did not run away at the end of the year.

I came back the next fall with even more problems weighting me down; but I decided that I was finished running away from problems and I started to confront them. At first, it was very painful and the results seemed slow in forth coming. However, I first noticed that people began to accept me more and more as I crawled out of my shell. I began to form solid relationships and not ones based on insincerity. I began to want to work hard, not just think I was working hard, and my grades slowly began to reflect such a change in attitude. I took my first step in emotional growth.

I started to look at my problems with my family, and they seemed smaller, and much more managable. I could talk to my father about my problems openly and also discuss his too. My mother's new family seemed so much less abrasive, and I could begin to accept them. I began to accept all problems, and understand that it was not just the problems at home that forced me away but some of the problems inside of me also. I saw that it was my fault too. I no longer needed a scape goat. I no longer needed to run.

Yes, he was accepted by William and Mary as well as the others.

A Bad One and a Good One, from the Same Underachiever

The first statement was written in early spring of her senior year; the second after she had been working for a few months and had time to think things over. The first one:

For 7 years I attended ——— a "magnet" school near my home. It seemed that the only attraction of this "magnet" was the TAG, or Talented and Gifted program. We students were rounded up and put in a room where we worked on long, laborious, and tedious projects and did "task cards"—problem-solving skills involved on an advanced level. I eventually dropped out of this program because it seemed to me that I hadn't been enriched a bit for it. Throughout my elementary school years I was placed in classrooms 2 or 3 grades above mine, and was ostracized for my abilities and my "weirdness." My grades were never top-notch. I believe this was because of social needs, depression, and dissatisfaction with my environment. I attended ———, a private Episcopalian preparatory institution, for 2 years after that. My grades improved greatly and I learned many things which still provoke my thoughts and interest, but I was extremely unhappy—both with the school and with my home life. Both the religious convictions of the school, its curriculum, and its staff, and the conservative, affluent condition of the student body contributed to my dissatisfaction. My parents had intended that I attend ——— through my graduation, but I felt my social life and mental health were being compromised in that environment; I enrolled at ——— senior high in 1984 as a TAG student. I believe that my previously inhibited and repressed feelings of individuality took control of my senses; I "acted out" my fantasies of being "wild" by skipping school, spiking my hair, and fighting constantly with my parents. Needless to say, my performance suffered greatly academically. This aberrance gradually diminished, and although my grades did not improve markedly, my attitude and manner became more contained; the recklessness of my freshman year dissipated into a strong penchant for fun and parties. I believe that my high school years have been, for the most part, debilitating to my intellect. The mediocrity with which I am surrounded is depressing, and academic excellence only accentuates the distance between the haves and have-nots in this school. TECH and TAG students are loaded with pressure from teachers and principals, who seem to merely seek prominence from their students' performances, and are taught that the only important knowledge is that which helps one pass standardized tests. Obviously, this scene does not pique my interest and motivate me to seek academic excellence. Therefore, I take from my classes that information I know to be relevant and important to my life, and that is enough for me. I don't believe I'll ever memorize facts for the sheer purpose of passing a test—I need to *feel* that I am learning for a purpose. I am very inquisitive, alert, and informed, and I will not hesitate to question that which I find hard to swallow. I am nervously certain that I will be a vibrant and active member of a college community—the *right* college community, however, is still rather hazy to me now. In the future, I plan on realizing and achieving many personal goals. I will do this armed with knowledge, integrity, and a strong will. I intend to leave this life having made a definite and unmistakable mark by changing that which is wrong, helping those who are ignored, and never hesitating to stand up for what I believe in.

That statement would have made anyone question whether she could function in college when everyone was out of step with her, no matter how praiseworthy her values and goals. But when school ended she got a telephone-answering job where she could see some of the legislative process in operation and some of her school dissatisfactions seemed smaller. Also, at that age, change comes faster than at any other time in life. After a few months, she wrote this one:

For the majority of my school years I agonized and fought against a system I felt was too impersonal and competitive, and I made things very hard for myself. I'm sure I confused most of my teachers by displaying high ability and low performance. I simply did not care for their methods of teaching and their lack of motivation. The competitive attitude of my fellow students intimidated me and I responded by displaying a lackadaisical, devil-may-care outlook on scholarly endeavors. If only I could find the right atmosphere, I thought and still do think, I would revive and perform to my ability. I have changed dramatically in my tastes and interests just in the last four years. Where once I found hard-core music and alarming clothes and hairstyles desirable, I now lean towards more mellow music and a less violent lifestyle. The anger I once felt toward the Establishment (embodied in the school system) has dissipated and been replaced with a yearning to see things change for the better so that today's children will have a more altruistic and caring environment and attitude in their school experience. The most important ingredient in any education, in my opinion, is a motivation to learn in order to help humankind . . . not make lots of money. While very few people of my age are certain of what they want their future to hold, I am gradually learning what I *don't* want—for instance, I definitely do not want to be employed in the food service business. I do not want to perform manual labor. I do not enjoy computers and mathematics, and while I love science in all its branches, the formulas and haze of numbers surrounding it frighten me a bit. On the other hand, I am beginning to learn more about what I do want. Politics fascinate me, and working on Capitol Hill this summer has given me great insight into the give-and-take personal politicking of our nation's Senate. While I have seen that much time is wasted on trivial matters such as quorums and the like while important bills on aid to the homeless wait, I think I am beginning to understand how things are done. It is frustrating, and this fascinates me even more. I have become active in the past six months regarding issues I feel are important. I have attended protests and done volunteer work for a few organizations and met many interesting and revolutionary people, and this has ignited the activist in me. I now have an outlet for my frustrations with the Establishment (now embodied in the government!) and I finally am doing something constructive with it. I never was interested in the "extracurricular activities" that seem so important to colleges these days. I preferred listening to twenty-year-old music and writing poetry to cheering at football games. I preferred reading books to joining the Math Club. I found the whole high school scene to be superficial and, frankly, useless in the great scheme of things. My attitude was, how can these people scream for a football team while nuclear war threatens our planet? This is extremist, I realize, and I probably missed some fun times. But I am glad I am this way. I believe the world needs more extremists, or the people cheering for the football team will never find out about acid rain and AIDS and homelessness. Well, that's the thumbnail sketch. Suffice it to say that I am different from my peers in many ways, and I intend to make lasting contributions in my lifetime to the betterment of my descendants.

The "right college" was one of those accepting her.

But beyond that, she courageously consented to let her essays be used as examples in the hope of helping others.

The Future Rewards of Doing a Good Job

One is not likely to think of the college application as anything more than a one-time chore. Wrong. It's a useful start on shaping yourself up for the job-hunting process after college. Today the application process is the most important aspect of job hunting. Employers are far more interested in the prospect's ability to think and to think clearly as evidenced by his ability to write and to speak well and how he works with others than they are in his grades, his major, or the name of the school he went to. As reported elsewhere in this book, several college investigating teams found that these were the qualities on which all kinds of employers, government and private, base their decisions. So, the agony and sweat invested now will help produce a better resume and a better interview four years hence; you've had some very valuable practice, and that practice will pay off.

14 🖋

The Interview?
Relax!

It Seldom Has Much Influence;
It Only Confirms Your Essays.

The sweaty palms, the tenseness, and the surging adrenaline are seldom necessary. Like the choice of major, the interview is one of the most overrated concerns in this whole college business. The number of colleges that require interviews is small and getting smaller, for a very good reason: unless it is an unusual case the interview is seldom going to reveal anything the admissions office doesn't already know from the application data and the recommendations. There are very few surprises.

To anxious teenagers it is probably impossible to overemphasize this point: the chances of an interview being the make-or-break element approach zero. What it is most likely to do is to confirm or lend support to the other evidence. Except for the rare cases when it can provide needed additional evidence, it is, like the vermiform appendix, pretty much the vestigial remnant of another time, little value in and a negligible influence on most admissions decisions. Nevertheless, admissions offices are daily filled with hopefuls expecting their interviews to make points toward acceptance. For the most part, they could spend the time more productively working on good application statements.

The person who most needs a good interview is hardly ever the one trying to improve his chances for a very selective school; he is the one needing to explain something in his past, how a parental divorce, for example, or an illness or his own attitudes affected his performance. These are some of the situations where an interview could—by filling in a missing part of the picture—make or break an admissions decision. But that has to be said guardedly, for a good interview could hardly overcome a bad application. What the applicant writes about himself is there in permanent black and white, where every member of the admissions committee, not just the person who interviewed him, can see it.

While most colleges still grant interviews, of the eight Ivies and three Little Ivies, for example, only Harvard requires one and it refers the applicant to a local alumnus. Some don't even mention interview in their admissions procedures. Many would abolish them entirely if they weren't afraid they'd be accused of a lack of interest, especially when the competition is giving them. Just stop to think: when a college is swamped with nearly five thousand applications, as Amherst and several others are, or eighteen thousand as the universities of Michigan and Virginia are, no admissions staff, even with student help, could possibly interview more than a fraction. Most public institutions don't bother. In Virginia's case, only about two thousand are interviewed, so in fairness to the other sixteen thousand, no interview notes go into applicants' files. Nevertheless, high school seniors flock to Charlottesville for the empty rite of a group session and tour.

Forty and fifty years ago, with a smaller population, the most selective colleges could offer interviews to most of the candidates, and many required them. Now they tend to make a difference only in the marginal cases or those where some unusual circumstance perhaps beyond the candidate's control has affected his record. For the vast majority of colleges an interview is simply not necessary. A good college that takes much over half of its applicants is going to take any and all who have good records and who write acceptable applications. Indeed, I tell most of my clients to forget about an interview when they visit a college and get on with the sampling and testing of the merchandise to find out whether it's right for them.

I do urge clients to seek interviews if they are marginal, if there's been a problem somewhere in the background and the admissions director would like to see the person himself, or if the college requires one. Otherwise, what new evidence is the college going to discover about this person? His academic record, his activities, what his teachers and perhaps an employer think about him are all on the record. And, what he has written about himself demonstrates how well he can think and express himself. With all that evidence in hand, it's going to be a rare candidate who surprises or who adds anything that changes the picture. However, much to my surprise many years ago, a client with a 2.6 grade point average got into a Grade A New England college partly because he interviewed as well as he wrote.

What Is a Good Interview?

A good interview is a good conversation. It is not an occasion for reviewing your resume, and certainly not for posturing, bragging, or faking. A good discussion means both parties are active contributors, that there's an exchange of ideas, that it's lively, that it ought to have some spontaneity and fun, that it can move easily from topic to topic and is not self-conscious. It may have nothing to do with the weighty business of college; it may be about baseball or reading or your or the interviewer's favorite topic. The candidate's poise or charm don't count. It's not the hairdo but what's under it.

How Does One Prepare?

The best preparation is one that enables you to come into the interview with an understanding of yourself and what you want out of college and out of—or of—life. If you know yourself you are talking from strength. Why? Because you are ready to respond to questions about yourself as if you knew what you were talking about. Further, you will be able to take conversational initiatives instead of merely reacting. Such self-knowledge is not a condition most teenagers find themselves in naturally. To achieve some measure of it, do the questioning of yourself suggested in the chapter on why you want to go to college; then you can meet the interviewer on even terms.

What Kinds of Questions Do They Ask?

Even if it's just as a courtesy, one is likely to be, "Do you have any questions?" You ought to have at least one that's of genuine interest to you, and one that will make him or her sit up and take notice. Some of mine would be: Are students here learning for the sake of learning or for grades? To what extent are the students involved in their own education, or are they largely lecture-listeners? What will this college do for me? Do students form friendships with faculty members? But don't ask questions that reveal you haven't done your homework; i.e., that you haven't looked at the catalog or the student guide they may have sent you.

The odds are they will ask what your interest is in their school, what you've done outside the classroom, what you've done with your summers, perhaps what you've read recently, or if you have some great interest.

Some interviewers are students, some professionals, some are good and some not; if you've done your homework on yourself you'll do very well.

An interview with an alumnus or alumna affords an opportunity to question one of the institution's products. It can supplement a college visit; he is some of the merchandise you can test. Look over the questions in the chapter on visits. What did the school do for him or her? Would the alum send his or her own child there? If he or she had it to do over would that college still be the choice? And so on.

Some Obvious Commonsense Tips

The only important thing about dress and hair is that they be neat.

You should look your interviewer in the eye, use his name, be positive, and be a lively conversational partner; but think, don't go off half-cocked. And no limp handshake!

Have a copy of your high school record with you.

And it goes without saying that honesty is not just the best policy; it is the only policy. Ditto for exaggeration, puffery, or poor manners; that way lies disaster.

As Dr. Faustus explained to his apprentice eager to have the secret: "Be honest if you would be eloquent."

15 ✍

If You've Made
a Mistake, You *Can*
Save Yourself

There's Always a Second Chance;
Don't Let Them Tell You Differently.

No matter what your mistake, you can correct it. Some mistakes can be shaken off without missing a beat; some may take a semester and some two semesters. The very worst ones might take longer. But no matter what it is, you have plenty of company; lots of others have made the same one and gotten back on the right track. Countless thousands get in the wrong places every year, and every college, except the most selective, does a brisk business in transfers. But those very selective ones don't have a monopoly on either quality or desirability.

This message of hope applies across the board to:

- freshmen who wanted to take a year off but whose parents made them go to college anyway,
- freshmen who are frustrated or miserable in the wrong college,
- students who've found they're in a professional program they don't like,

221

- flunkouts,
- dropouts,
- even students convicted of crimes.

The American college establishment is so big and so diverse that everyone can get a second and sometimes even a third chance. In no other country can a youth have so many different opportunities.

But because he doesn't know any better, and colleges sometimes misinform him, the student in the wrong pew or the erring one often thinks he can't improve his situation or save himself. He almost always can; religion isn't the only place where there's grace and redemption.

This doesn't necessarily apply to the person just looking for greener grass on the other side of the fence; the one who thinks a bigger, more urban place or more prestigious name would be better; nor to the one whose social life isn't what she thinks it ought to be (a principal, but usually temporary, cause of girls wanting to transfer). A freshman at Columbia, for example, who yearns to transfer to Harvard—or another equally selective school—might as well put it out of his mind. Illustrative was the experience of a Columbia freshman with a 3.6 average who wanted to transfer to Harvard, which had turned him down as a high school senior, despite an outstanding scholastic record and the editorship of the school paper to his credit. "All my life," he said, "I've been doing the things that Harvard wanted." But it was to no avail; hordes of others had been doing the same thing.

The facts of life are that the most selective schools have so little attrition that the competition for what few transfer openings there are is two to five times greater than for freshman places. In fact, some—Dartmouth and Carleton, for example—don't even take transfers. A few years ago, after I had told the Oberlin admissions director about a prospect with two solid years of straight As who had outgrown her college, he said they'd be glad to "consider" her. I said, "You must not have heard me;

she has two years of straight As." He said, "This year we've got at least three hundred applicants for twenty places and I'd guess nearly half of them have straight As." But she did get in.

The Transfer Market for the Unhappy Student in Good Standing

As the Oberlin case indicates, the transfer market varies; in some years when a lot of students were taking a year off they would have come through the telephone after her. Since 1986, it has been more difficult to transfer into good, but not very selective, colleges than to get in as a freshman. In 1987, for instance, it took a C+ to a B− average to transfer into some colleges that were taking high school seniors with good C averages. These colleges just haven't been having as much attrition as they did five or ten years earlier. Unlike the situation a few years ago, good colleges in the South and Midwest are also having less attrition, but these two regions still contain most of the bargains and are where an unhappy student should find the quality and the ambience he's seeking.

Below a C Average? Don't Let Them Tell You There's No Hope.

If an unhappy student has an average below a C, he may think he's stuck because a registrar or some other official has told him no other college will look at him. That just ain't so, but unfortunately, students often are told this and as a result don't try. There always are other options. If you're mired in engineering or some other professional program and hating it, or aren't making your grades because you just don't like the place, don't let anyone tell you that you can't get in anywhere else. You can. You don't have to be stuck with a bad marriage.

And that doesn't mean you'll have to take less or settle for Podunk. However, you may have to do penance of some sort. Often passing a couple of summer school courses or doing a term or a year's good work will demonstrate the motivation the admissions officer is looking for. Or, he may want you to raise your grade point average to a C overall. Then you'll have several suitable choices. Those tasks may take some extra time, but that's not the worst thing in the world, as we shall see a little further on.

The Student in College Against His Will

The youth whose parents made him or her go when he wanted to take a year off and who is failing should get out right now and work a year or two until he's ready to go. As pointed out in the Twenty Myths chapter, staying in school under duress only aggravates the problem. In thirty years, as a college official or as a counselor, I have never known a kid to do well when he's been pushed into going.

Even if he's not failing, the discontent is more likely than not to breed trouble in the months ahead in poor performance and the accompanying dissatisfaction. It's likely to prove a waste of time and money as well. He's better off getting out as soon as possible and doing something else while the maturing process does its work.

The Flunkout CAN Rescue Himself.

A typical example this summer was a youth who had been academically suspended for a year by a school he heartily disliked. He was happy to hear that three colleges said they'd accept him, particularly because an official at his college had told him that not only would no school take him, but that he couldn't get credit for any work done in the suspension year. He had spent the term after his dismissal proving himself by carrying a full course load at the local community college, making good grades, and holding a job besides. All three colleges said they would give him credit for the community college work. The moral: since most college officials know very little about the rules of most other institutions, make your own inquiries. If anything, the kind of counseling a student gets in college is often worse than that received in high school, for this sort of case turns up year after year. And there would undoubtedly be many more examples like this if failing students refused to be brainwashed.

Even if this young man hadn't made the effort to prove he meant business, he could have had several options because there are always reputable colleges that need students. True, a student is not legal tender in the academic world if he doesn't have a C average or isn't eligible to return to his own college, but there are a lot of good admissions officers willing to give him a second chance, particularly if he had a good high school record and there are extenuating circumstances, such as being in the wrong program or in a clearly unsuitable school. The latter happens most frequently when the parents have insisted on making the college choice, or on making the youth go when he didn't want to. An unscientific guess would be that half the unhappy choices are the parents' fault.

I have always found plenty of admissions directors to be sympathetic when it seemed obvious that the student either made a bad choice or that his parents pushed him into it when he either wanted to take a year off or go somewhere else. The student who makes the effort to change almost always winds up in a college he likes better and therefore profits from. It's useful to remember that admissions officers have common sense and are understanding. They're perfectly willing to bend or break the establishment's rules if there's a legitimate reason to do so, which usually means a reasonable expectation that the applicant will prosper with a change of scenery.

Sometimes the School Is Partly to Blame.

When it seems clear a student's troubles may be all or partly his college's fault, an admissions director may finesse the rule that a student should be eligible to return to his original school. Several summers ago, for example, a young man came to me whose grades at Johns Hopkins had been going steadily downhill for three years and he'd been dismissed. He was a quiet, unassertive biology major unhappily caught in a mass-production, cutthroat premed competition. He was vaguely aware that his educational experience might be one-dimensional but he had gotten no help or counseling from any adviser or teacher for three years. He had doubts about what he was doing and about himself. Invariably, anyone in trouble as a junior rings alarm bells, because it looks as if his pattern has been set. But this young man had made an outstanding high school record or he wouldn't have met Hopkins's intense admissions competition in the sciences. Wooster's admissions office agreed that this fellow was a victim and in the wrong school, and admitted him for the fall term. He made the Dean's List for three semesters at Wooster and went on to graduate school.

The All-F Flunkout: A Rehabilitation Case

The person who flunks out just for lack of effort gets little sympathy. He's going to have to prove he means business. If he has failed his freshman year, he might do it with good grades in a community college for one semester. If he flunks out as a sophomore, the skepticism will be greater and so will the demands on him. If it happens as a junior, he's in real trouble and might be well advised to stay out and work a year or two and get his priorities in order.

The Dropout from High School or College

The most dramatic example in my experience of how open the door is for high school dropouts was a client who had quit high school in the ninth grade but who was a strong contender for a major fellowship as a college senior. After five years out of school, he took the General Educational Development test, passed it, and went to college and was on the Dean's List most of his time there. As the chapter on Twenty Myths points out, a high school diploma isn't needed to get into a good college.

The college dropout can always get back in if he's in good standing, but if he wants to return to the place he started, he'd be wise to make plans with the college before he leaves.

However, even if he never goes back he can still have a rich, full life and do great things. One of the shining examples I know is a man who made a fortune by age forty-two, retired to become a full-time bibliophile, and has for years been a celebrated benefactor of the prestige university he never got his degree from.

The Student in the Wrong Program

A change of program may often mean a change of scenery. A disaffected student in architecture at Cornell, for example—as one young friend was—isn't likely to get into another Ivy League school or another department at his own school. That young man was in limbo, unable to transfer to the College of Arts and Sciences because he didn't have a C average in architecture: he was caught in the watertight compartmentalization of the university bureaucracy. But since he had a first-rate high school record and it was obvious that he'd gotten himself in the wrong curriculum, he was able to get into a first-rate college.

Similarly, a creative youth who had the idea that engineering would be the perfect preparation for design, found Georgia Tech to be a tough grind and an assembly line of huge classes where the teachers were either unavailable or were foreigners barely able to speak English. He also found he didn't like engineering. He had only a 1.6 average at the end of his freshman year, but he took a couple of summer school courses to prove he was on track, and was able to get into a good college, one infinitely more likely to develop his creative instincts.

Another who chose engineering, at Tulane, thinking that was the route to becoming a flier, found in his freshman year that he was not enamored of the field. In family conferences at the end of that year and midway into the next, Puritan values prevailed and it was decided that he should stick it out, although his interest, his morale, and his grades all were sagging. But like the fellow at Cornell, he couldn't transfer out to Arts and Sciences because he didn't have a C average. Since he'd had a good high school record, however, and it was clear his was a case of being in the wrong pew, three collges said they'd take him. Two other good ones did after he got an A and a B in two summer school courses. So he wound up with his choice of three first-rate schools and two good ones.

The prospect of having to spend a semester or a year to be born again should not inspire dread reactions that your life is being truncated or somehow damaged. After all, the goal is to improve your situation and your long-term outlook. Teenagers nevertheless think the worst and will continue to, because of a paradox of adolescence: a conviction of immortality cohabiting with a certainty they'll be over the hill by age twenty-one and that a whole year blocked out of that brief interim is just too much. A fine example of this teenage syndrome was cited in Chapter 3, by the high school senior who said, "Well, anyway it's four years out of my life," but as a senior at Stanford was "aghast" to be told he'd said it.

And Some Have Been Convicted of Crimes.

I have had clients who have been convicted of various crimes and who have been accepted by and prospered in colleges; the question to be answered, naturally, is whether the person is now on track and seems likely to lead a law-abiding life. In one of many different kinds of cases, a college sophomore convicted of helping to steal two cases of wine intended for a faculty dinner got into another college. As is so often the case, the violation turned out to be a searing learning experience.

Two Important Things to Remember

In almost every case everywhere, the grades go down when the morale does. As a consequence, here are two vital injunctions to heed:

One, continue to work hard. If you decide to transfer, the better the grades are, the easier it will be. If the grade point average falls below the waterline C, the problem is made more difficult.

Two, get out as soon as you can. Don't aggravate your troubles by sticking with a bad situation. As a former Oberlin dean said, "If you're on the wrong train, get off at the first stop."

16 ✍

How to Judge a
Private Counselor

Investigate Thoroughly or
Risk Doing More Harm Than Good.

What do you expect a private counselor to do for your child that the high school counselor isn't doing or that you're afraid he or she can't do?

Do you want an edge to get into a very selective school, advice on the academic program, help in finding and getting into the best and most suitable college, help for a child with a learning problem, vocational guidance or testing, or something else? Some of those are valid reasons; some are will-o-the-wisps or unnecessary.

No private counselor is going to get your son or daughter into Harvard or Princeton. Indeed, some colleges won't pay any attention to him or her.

A good counselor is a knowledgeable adviser and advocate, presenting, defending, or sometimes pushing the student with the admissions officer. But that can go only so far. Unless the kid's family has given the school a lot of money, the admissions officer is going to make a professional decision and what the applicant himself has done will speak far louder than any other voice. In fact, when it gets down to the wire, that is the only voice. So, the best that anyone can do is to help the student present himself to the best advantage. If he is a junior or rising senior the most a counselor can do is to advise as solid an academic program as possible and involvement in outside activities.

By helping the student see what it is he wants to say in his application statements, a competent counselor can perform the function of a good editor or rhetoric instructor, enlightening him to present himself as effectively as possible. In very competitive situations—as noted in the chapter on a good application—this is crucial because it is the place where one can set himself apart from all the others who have records as good or better.

But no ghost writing. The adviser's job is to help the student see and be himself. Personal statements written by a hired hand won't work if the admissions office is on its toes. And as noted in the chapter on application essays, many a meddling parent has hung his child. A student who has done a good job on his personal statements is also going to handle that vastly overrated bugaboo, the interview, much more confidently and skillfully.

Many parents go to a private counselor for a very good reason: to seek out a range of intelligent choices in a day when college costs can easily go over $15,000 a year and the schools (meaning you, the taxpayer and PTA member) don't make the costly effort to provide knowledgeable college advice. This is where good help can be worthwhile, but the adviser's criteria should be much more than the client's grades, class rank, and test scores. He should know more about the colleges than their freshman profiles. He should be able to suggest places where the person interested in ideas or the one interested in causes or in things would fit. He should be able to suggest schools where students with learning disabilities have had successful experiences, not just consult directories. The mere fact that an institution has a program for the learning-disabled doesn't mean that its students pass their courses. There is a lot of lip service in scores of catalogs that needs to be checked out for truth in advertising.

The counselor's objective, in other words, is to try to make a match that will make a difference in the student's life. To be able to do this he also has to know something about the child and his family: is it a happy or a broken home; does this kid live in the shadow of an achieving sibling or parent? And he has to get the child's confidence and trust. What hope does an overworked high school counselor have of doing this, especially when he or she may see a student only in glancing encounters, if at all, in four years?

What About Testing?

When a prospective client asks me if I do any aptitude or vocational testing I say no, that kids have been tested up one side and down the other for twelve school years, and unless it's a case for a psychiatrist, a psychologist, or a speech or reading therapist, the chances are that nothing very new or useful will be learned. If it's a learning disability it *should* have been uncovered long before the student reached the eleventh grade. Similarly, even allowing for the natural abrasion between adolescents and parents, a personality problem should have revealed itself before then.

The concern for aptitude testing usually tells more about the parents than the student: they're worried because he or she isn't getting good grades or doesn't know what career direction to be thinking about.

Such a test may be an interesting exercise, and it may relieve the parents, so if the family wants to spend money that way, fine, but it's not likely to affect the course of a teenager's life. When a family has had their child so tested I always suggest waiting until after the interview to look at it. Invariably, the interests or abilities that have been elicited in the interview are the same ones they've paid $150 or more to identify. More important is the thread that runs through this book: the teenager doesn't know what will engage him twenty years hence, and the things that will determine what kind of person he will be haven't happened to him yet.

Who Are These Private Counselors?

The panic to get into college in the fifties spawned the first generation of private counselors who saw a chance to cash in on the demand for help in getting into the "right" college. Some traded on having been high school counselors or on having worked in an admissions office, but they, like most of the others, knew little or nothing about colleges or what a good college experience should be, much less how to try to make a good match of student and college. The threat of going to Vietnam brought the next crop. Advisers sprang up everywhere to get sons into the college draft haven. Both times a changing market drove most of them out of business.

Today the metropolitan areas are full of them again; some admissions officers think the number is larger than ever and still growing. Most of them are no more qualified than their predecessors, and many colleges refuse to deal with them for good reason: they know nothing about colleges. Like selling magazines, anyone can get into it. There could not ever be a degree in college counseling; competence is gained only by long experience. And there are no legally required standards. Many a housewife has called to ask my help in starting what seems an easy and attractive business, especially if she's had a course in counseling. One client, a retired bureaucrat wholly innocent of any competence in the area, set himself up as a college counselor in a Washington suburb. Incidentally, when his son was unhappy at the university the son had chosen against my advice, the father turned to me for help. So the word is, buyer beware.

Some Suggestions on Checking Out a Counselor

The first thing to do, obviously, is to ask for references and check out some of his former clients. Ask them if they'd send their other children to this person. If you can't get references, forget it!

Also, before spending the several hundred dollars, call one or two of the colleges your child is interested in and ask the admissions officers if they have dealt with this counselor, whether they still will, and if not, why.

Ask the counselor where he or she went to college. This has a status-conscious smell but is relevant. If it was a rigorous, high quality institution, that's a good sign. If it was a place mainly in the business of preparing teachers, whether big or small, that's a loud warning signal. Teacher-training institutions are vocationally oriented places of low standards hardly likely to acquaint anyone with a demanding intellectual experience. If it was a university, particularly one easy to get into, that's also a warning. Unless he was in an honors program he probably wouldn't have had the benefit of being involved in his own education, of living in a community of shared values and expectations, or of a continuing dialogue with teachers.

Ask about professional background:

—How long has he or she been doing this?

—What was the preparation? Neither a degree in counseling nor years as a high school counselor is relevant. Undergraduate counseling courses are more shadow than substance, and no graduate course can impart common sense or intelligence, much less any knowledge of colleges. As for high school counselors, when was the last time your school board budgeted $100,000 or so for travel so guidance counselors could make working-day visits to colleges? Unless school systems beef up their guidance staffs and balloon the budgets the counselors can't do the essential homework.

One example of the consequent guidance that is epidemic

is that of a girl with a 2.6 average at a selective girls' school whose counselor recommended Cornell, Penn, Davidson, Duke, North Carolina State, and the University of Maryland. Considerations of suitability aside—and none were—she couldn't have gotten into any one of the first four and the other two were safeties resulting from the counselor's ineptitude.

Nor is having been on a college admissions staff any indication of expertise. That only means the person knows something about one institution. And it is common practice for brand-new graduates to serve in a college's admissions office a year or two for an interim job.

What is to the point is how many colleges the counselor has investigated as described in the chapter on visiting one. Group tours don't count, whether conducted by the institution or not. Neither does a visit talking to the sales staff in admissions. The test is, what can he tell you about the institution, its mores, the kind of people it produces, the atmosphere?

Membership in a Professional Group

This is no guarantee. There is a group, the Independent Educational Counselors Association, that now asks applicants for membership for their experiences and how many colleges they've visited in the last year, which is an important step in the right direction, but its membership is a mixed bag.

What Does the Counselor Claim to Do?

Is he saying he will get your child in college, smooth the path, help with applications, instruct for the interview, find the school right for your child's career interests? Is he saying he will match the student and college? If so, how? What are his criteria?

If he advertises that "with our help" you can get into a "desired school, get grant and loan money," beware!

A competent counselor will help the student find a college that will help him grow, not one with a major that holds his adolescent interest. Those who start out with clear goals and never change their major are those least likely to graduate, a North Carolina study found, while those who changed four times were most likely to finish. Besides, as we've said at every possible pretext, practically no mature adult's work has any connection with his freshman choice of major.

So, beware the counselor who promises to find an institution that has a very good program in just the specialty your child is interested in today.

A competent counselor will help the student look at himself a little more clearly. A competent counselor will ask the kinds of questions that will elicit the student's values, goals, and interests and how he looks at himself in relation to the world, not whether he wants this or that program.

Ask the counselor if he uses the Gourman Report. If he does, he hasn't been clued in and doesn't know what he's doing. The Gourman Report, an off-the-wall compendium of meaningless statistics, is a fraudulent thing because it purports to rate institutions numerically on idiotic criteria the author picks while sitting in his little office. He has no supporters in the academic world. The first one in 1967 was ignored; a much more ambitious third one nearly twenty years later has gotten some publicity and some high school counselors have taken it seriously, which is too bad because it can do harm.

In short, a good counselor should have good rapport with and knowledge of the student and his family, and should be a person who inspires trust in his character and common sense and confidence in his knowledge. Just as you wouldn't choose a doctor who promised to cure you or a lawyer who assured you he'd win your case, beware the so-called counselor who makes such come-on claims.

17 ✍

Some Truths About Financial Aid

Be Wary of the Modern Sellers of Wooden Nutmegs.

"A lot of people don't get financial aid," a college vice president complained to me several years ago, "because they don't ask for it. They assume that because they're in the income range of thirty thousand to fifty thousand a year they're not eligible, when as a matter of fact they often are eligible." He wouldn't have that particular complaint today. With college costs soaring well into five digits, almost everybody's seeking aid, and the average income of aid recipients is rising. One recent year, 40 percent of Dartmouth's scholarships went to families in the $30,000 to $50,000 range; at Case Western Reserve, the average income was $45,000—which meant as many over that figure as under. At Oberlin, 32 percent had incomes of $45,000 and over; one as high as $116,000. And a study of thirty-two of the top colleges and universities in 1988 revealed that 21 percent of their aid recipients came from families with incomes over $60,000, quite a big jump from the 8 percent in that bracket in 1984.

Today, that vice president would have two different complaints. One would be that parents are falling victim to yet another myth about colleges—that applying for aid imperils the chances of acceptance. The other would be that families aren't being smart in another way: they're not asking the best, most reliable source of help. That source is the college, not a private advisory service.

The Reagan administration cutbacks in student aid, rising college costs, and the 1987 and 1988 upward blip in applications all conspired to incubate rumors in some suburbias that, other things beings equal, the college was going to accept the full-paying student and reject the one who needed aid. Therefore, went the rationale, struggle through the first year without help, if possible; then, once safely in, ask for aid for the next year.

This myth flies in the face of common sense. Good colleges are competing as aggressively as they can for a relatively small, and shrinking, pool of good applicants. They would be crippling themselves in the competition if they were simply to favor those who could pay their way. Even a cursory check of a directory will reveal that in most private colleges, a half to two thirds, or even three quarters, of the students are on financial aid. At Harvard, for example, it's 70 percent.

The truth is that the financial aid director of any good college will be only too glad to say, if a parent will only take the trouble to telephone him, that (1) the rumor is 95 percent hokum, and (2) the tactic of not applying for aid until the sophomore year is likely to be self-defeating. He will also be glad to reveal whether asking for aid influences any admissions decisions, and if so, how, and which ones.

The College Scholarship Service, a part of the College Board, did a survey in the mid-eighties to discover whether or not most decisions were aid-blind. Executive Director Hal F. Higginbotham said only a smattering of colleges deviated from a strictly aid-blind policy, and they tended to be in the wait-list decisions. Most of the better colleges, he said, have made internal budget decisions to commit sufficient resources to attract the best class they can, and the decisions that aren't aid-blind are marginal ones. The competition for that small pool of good applicants dictates that they follow such a policy, and he added that four years after their survey there was no evidence to the contrary. Anyway, if it's not a selective college, whose acceptances aren't aid-blind, it's not to worry; there are plenty of others eager to provide aid as well as acceptance.

Jim White, Oberlin's financial aid director, was even more emphatic. The good colleges, he agreed, aren't influenced by need, except after the aid money has been exhausted and it comes down to deciding on the tail end of the applicant pool, the last 5 or 10 percent. And they usually involve cases that are unusual or marginal.

Both said the delayed-aid tactic was highly suspect. Hal Higginbotham said, "The parent runs a difficult risk." The college makes assumptions that aid requests are going to remain pretty constant in each cohort; then if a new one pops up the second year, it raises a red flag. Jim White said, "If they haven't applied for aid the freshman year, it raises questions, so a request the second year will get a thorough investigation."

So the moral is, don't take a chance; apply for aid early. What's more, in the very, very unlikely event that an aid request affects a decision in a selective college, there's always at least one other just as good where it won't. But the student or the parents can eliminate the anxiety at the start by telephoning the financial aid office and asking a few questions. You should get straight answers and you won't be running any risk of penalizing yourself.

That college vice president's other complaint today would be that parents are going to the wrong places for help in getting aid because the combination of rising costs and government aid cutbacks has spawned a new cottage industry. Easy bucksters are promising to find scholarships with computer-assisted searches, to fill out forms, or to help the family do what they call "beating the system." Much of this is a modern version of the medieval entrepreneur's holy relics and papal pardons or the early American peddlers' wooden nutmegs. One of their come-ons is that hundreds of millions, or billions, of aid money goes unused each year. That will-o'-the-wisp has been flitting around for thirty-five years that I know of. Most of this sum is fantasy: neither you nor anyone you know could qualify for a dollar of it. It's money available only to employees of certain firms, it's for grants to students interested in a particular subject who live in a specific town, or it's in church, union, garden club, fraternal or other local grants, and they are usually trifling sums. As Jim White said, "If it's not being used, it's because it can't be used."

The fact is that at least 95 percent of all aid is, and always has been, available through the colleges. It follows that the best place to ask for help is the college's financial aid officer. He not only is the best informed, but contrary to what you might be told by one of these new entrepreneurs or by too-frequent newspaper or magazine articles, he has a vested interest in helping you. Why? The admissions office may admit you and it's his job to try to make it possible for you to enroll.

Equally important is the kind of person the aid director is. Most of them are in this kind of work because they're people who want to help; by profession they're givers. The last thing likely to occur to them would be to set up a "system" that you have to try to crack or beat. Naturally there are rules that make sense, and in the reputable colleges the aid directors play the game straight and by the rules. As Sandra Gray, until recently financial aid director at Johns Hopkins noted, "We want to meet a student's full need. The whole basis of our job is to help." So far as Federally funded programs go, she emphasized, "We're not holding back; we have to give it back to the government if we don't spend it, so we lose it if we hold back."

Furthermore, if the family thinks the aid package is too small and that everything hasn't been taken into consideration, all they have to do is appeal it and if the claim is valid, an adjustment will be made. Ms. Gray said, "We make adjustments in most cases, probably 95 percent."

All of that help, from people who want to help, is free.

The second best place *should be* the high school guidance office; if it's not, raise cain with your school board. That is also free.

The Federal programs—mostly loans, and to be listed later on—account for the great bulk of financial aid, and *all* of them are available through the college financial aid officer. And if you live in a state that gives grants or loans, any good aid officer will know all about them and be able to advise on eligibility and how to get them even if they're not channelled through his office because his school is in a different state.

In addition, the colleges themselves have their own scholarship and loan funds. However, if they don't have the loan funds or the installment payment plans you need, the aid officer can and will tell you where to ask.

Computer-assisted searches are likely to cost you more than you'll get. Case Western's financial aid director Don Chennell paid for several applicants' searches and not one got a dollar he or she wouldn't have gotten by applying to the aid office. In California, searches were paid for two thousand applicants and only one got anything the colleges wouldn't have offered him voluntarily and at no cost. And that one got only $500.

At Oberlin, where two thirds of its four thousand-plus applicants may ask for help, Aid Director Jim White said he's never come across one who found aid from a computer search. Furthermore, he said, not one of those computer-search outfits has ever asked him what Oberlin has in the way of aid, and Oberlin is one of the best-endowed and wealthiest colleges in the country. As do many of her colleagues, Claire Matthews, Connecticut College dean of admissions and former associate director of financial aid at Wesleyan University, gets practically apoplectic on the subject of private financial aid advisers. All they do, she says, is sell information available from colleges for the asking or that's in state or U.S. Department of Education or College Entrance Examination Board publications.

The Department of Education publishes an annual *Student Guide* describing all the financial aid programs, as well as how and where to apply. It also provides the Federal aid application form, and an eighty-four-page book listing private sources of aid. Although titled *Higher Education Opportunities for Minorities and Women,* it applies also to non-minority males. All of these publications are free and should be available in every high school guidance office in the land. If they're not, the guidance office isn't doing its job, and you the taxpayer should demand better service from your hired help.

If you still have questions after reading the Department's booklets, it has a toll-free Student Aid Information Center that will answer them. The number is 1-800-INFO, and it operates from 9 A.M. to 5:30 P.M., Eastern Standard Time, Monday through Friday.

Every guidance office should also have the free booklets from the College Board and from the American College Testing Program, which not only have information on aid programs but which also enable parents to calculate what they're likely to have to contribute toward college costs.

For $12.95, *The College Cost Book,* also published by the College Board, will answer just about every question families can ask, will lead them through the aid process, and in addition will tell them the total costs of any college they're interested in: tuition, room and board, books and supplies, transportation, and incidentals.

Parents may think that a private adviser will give them an edge in getting aid money and will help "market" the student. True, a financial adviser might suggest buying a new car or some other purchase to reduce assets, or increasing retirement contributions to reduce income, or giving gifts of securities to grandparents rather than to children because students' assets are taxed at a higher rate than the parents' are, but these are things anyone who reads the financial aid forms carefully could hardly fail to deduce.

But no financial advisory service is going to "market" a student to any good college. The student markets himself with his record of achievements—both in and out of class—and by what he says about himself in his personal statements. Those things speak so loudly and so clearly that no pro like an admissions officer (who's read thousands of applications) is going to be conned by some johnny-come-lately-third-party's put-in.

If an advisory service says it will find you colleges where your son or daughter can get a scholarship because he or she has SAT scores totaling 900 or a B average, beware. It's perfectly true that the woods are full of such discounts, but most of those colleges are themselves discount merchandise that I would not recommend to a strong C student, much less a B student. As *College Cost* observes, it amounts to getting discount coupons on something you don't want to buy anyway.

And if someone tells you that you can use such an offer as leverage to get more aid from another, better school, forget it. The better school isn't going to buy. There may be some who will, but I have never heard of one who would. That of course doesn't apply to the area of athletic scholarships, the academic world's red light district, where the soliciting constitutes a dread social and educational disease. If the college admits you— which means it wants you—it is going to give you all the aid you qualify for; and as Ms. Gray pointed out, if you can show that you deserve more than the package you've been offered, the aid officer will no doubt make an adjustment, giving more grant and less loan, or more overall.

All that is not to say that all aid packages will be identical. So far as government aid is concerned, they will be, but institutions of comparable quality may not have equal-size kitties of their own grant monies, so one college may be able to give a larger scholarship and thus a smaller loan to be repaid. The thing to do here is to decide whether a smaller cost today is as important as the educational experience's lifelong effect. As with most things, cost is soon forgotten when the purchase gives satisfaction.

If someone tells you he can save you several thousand dollars by this kind of shopping, beware the bait-and-switch game; the loss in quality is almost certainly going to be much greater. Scads of colleges will pay the full freight for a National Merit Scholar or perhaps as much as full tuition for A students with high SATs, but at most of them a good student wouldn't have anyone to have a serious conversation with, except for an occasional faculty member.

Well over half of the colleges—about twelve hundred—have no-need, or merit, scholarships, and most of them are for the very top students or are so competitive that it would be much easier to get into Stanford or Harvard than to win one. For example, a client outstanding enough to get into MIT failed to win one in Washington University's competition. Another, accepted at two very selective New England colleges was able to win only one of the lesser, $2,000 scholarships at the College of Wooster. Case Western Reserve offers a textbook illustration. Here, twelve hundred hopefuls take an all-morning exam that is tougher than the SAT and go through an interview to try to win one of nineteen scholarships.

In case you think I'm exaggerating, here are a couple of the easier questions from Wooster's exam:

—"Assume that bioengineers will perfect a great variety of synthetic organs; even assume that parts of the brain will be replaced by synthetic devices. At what point does the recipient of numerous synthetic organs or mechanical devices cease to be human? Is there a boundary line separating 'being human' from 'being not human' but merely 'human-like' in the sense of being composed of synthetic organs, tissue, and artificial blood?"

—"Choose any two historical revolutions which on first glance appear quite dissimilar as historical phenomena. Why are they both called 'revolutions'?"

Similarly, the National Merit Scholarships are won by only about 7,000 of each year's 2.5 million high school seniors, and no financial advisory service can help there, just a well-sharpened brain.

Anyone who thinks a private adviser is going to uncover the rich grants should know about the experience of the college that probably offers more no-need scholarships in proportion to its size than any in the country. It is Wabash, a first-rate men's college in Indiana, where over 70 percent of the seniors go on to graduate school. While 83 percent of the 775 students get some kind of aid, *nearly 30 percent* have merit awards worth about $4,500 a year. That is an astoundingly high figure. Not one of these was obtained with the help of an private adviser. And financial aid director James Baer is not interested in talking to private advisers. The students' achievements in high school and in the community do the job. Wabash is a school that has been fortunate in being a darling of the Eli Lilly and other foundations.

With few exceptions, winners of merit awards demonstrate a good deal more than straight A averages and 1400 SATs. They're not just bright; they're the really able.

Even if the financial aid form shows a family doesn't qualify for aid, campus jobs are available on most campuses. Some few restrict the jobs to aid recipients, but even when that is the case, the competition for jobs in town is much less. Since many of them start at $4 per hour, a freshman working fifteen hours a week can make a contribution of over $2,000 for the school year. Later on if he has a more skilled job at a higher rate the figure will be much larger.

How Aid Is Given

It is part grant, part loan, and part job. How much of each depends on the family's need. The greater the need, the larger the grant part is likely to be. The size of the grant may also be affected by how much money the college itself can spend for this purpose, and whether the student qualifies for a scholarship awarded on merit. Grant money from Federal funds is given on a need basis, which is determined by what the figures in the financial aid form show.

The Process

1. The family fills out and sends in to the College Scholarship Service its Financial Aid Form, or to the American College Testing Service its Family Financial Statement. The college will say which one it wants. The high school guidance office supplies the forms.

It is important to check the boxes applying for Federal aid; otherwise you may not qualify for anything.

2. These agencies follow a Federal formula to arrive at a family contribution figure based on the family's assets and income. The theory is that this is what a family should be contributing to the child's support, whether at school or at home.

Another processing determines eligibility for Federal and state grants.

3. Copies of the results are sent to the family and to the colleges the family has indicated.

4. The college's financial aid officer determines how much need-based help the student will get.

How the Aid Package Is Assembled

First a Pell grant is given if the family has a low enough income to qualify, usually well under $25,000, then a Supplemental Educational Opportunity Grant if there's exceptional need. Any state grants come next. Then the college may award grant money out of its own funds.

Next come loans. For the 5 percent Perkins and the 8 percent Stafford Federal loans, need must be shown. Any state loans are also part of this slice. The Federal PLUS or SLS loans do not require a show of need but the borrower may have to undergo a credit analysis. Last come any college or private loans.

The third part of the package is a campus job under the Federal College Work-Study Program. Most colleges limit the number of hours to twelve or fifteen, on the theory that college ought to be a full-time endeavor.

And even if you don't qualify for aid, a campus or a town job—which the student seeks after he gets there—can reduce the cost appreciably, besides providing the important function of letting the youth work for part of his or her own education.

The financial aid director is no stern nay-saying bureaucrat; quite the opposite. So far as the rules allow, he's trying to make it easier for you. So, whatever you think your chances are, apply. You'll never know unless you ask.

Afterword

And Now . . .

I rest my case by reproducing the message of a now yellowed and brittle clipping torn out of *The Chronicle of Higher Education* way back in 1982. The fact that the article was written, not by an educator, but by the Omaha, Nebraska, owner of a scrap-metal business, attests to its real-world validity. It has the stamp of universality; what he says applies with equal force to those who would be doctors, lawyers, engineers, scientists, or financial or industrial magnates. Its message was as true in 1982 as it was in 1882 or 1782 (witness Benjamin Franklin and Thomas Jefferson, America's first Renaissance men), and it will be recognized doctrine in the no-holds-barred, entrepreneurial worlds of 1992 and 2002, for this maverick businessman's ideas speak of eternal verities.

Such other evidence in the book as the Haverford and Oberlin College and the University of Virginia alumni surveys gives consumer testimony to the value of a liberal education in fields far removed from their majors. This, from the venture capitalist employer's side, offers pungent proof that the life-giving message for everyone thinking about college is that what counts is

251

empowerment of abilities and character. Neither the choice of major nor the name of the college that so concern you now will make much difference. The *Chronicle*, the highly respected academic news journal, has never published a more cogent argument from any professor, provost, or president.

LIBERAL ARTS MAJORS PROVE SPECIALIZATION ISN'T REQUIRED FOR SUCCESS IN BUSINESS
by Sam Bittner

I have owned a scrap-metal business for 35 years. A year ago, I hired a new manager with unusual qualifications. He has an educational background of history and English; he holds a master's degree in foreign languages, and he speaks French and German fluently.

He knew nothing about the scrap-metal business. I gave him one week of instruction, and told him to make mistakes and then use intelligence, imagination, and logic. He has turned this into one of the most efficiently run metal industries in the Middle West.

My company took a contract to extract beryllium from a mine in Arizona. I called in several consulting engineers and asked, "Can you furnish a chemical or electrolytical process that can be used at the mine site to refine directly from the ore?" Back came a report saying I was asking for the impossible—a search of the computer tapes had indicated that no such process existed.

I paid the engineers for their report. Then I hired a student from Stanford University who was home for the summer. He was majoring in Latin American history with a minor in philosophy.

I gave him an airplane ticket and a credit card and told him, "Go to Denver and research the Bureau of Mines archives and locate a chemical process for the recovery of beryllium." He left on Monday. I forgot to tell him that I was sending him for the impossible.

He came back on Friday. He handed me a pack of notes and booklets and said, "Here is the process. It was developed 33 years ago at a government research station at Rolla, Mo." He then continued, "And here also are other processes for the recovery of mica, strontium, columbium, and yttrium, which also exist as residual ores that contain beryllium." After one week of research he was making sounds like a metallurgical expert.

He is now back in school, but I am keeping track of him. When other companies are interviewing the engineering and the business-administration mechanics, I'll be there looking for that history-and-philosophy major.*

During the past year, I, like every other businessman, was looking for new sources of financing because of the credit crunch created by the interest market. I located my new sources. I simply hired a journalism student and gave him an assignment to write a report titled, "The Availability of Money and Credit in the United States."

These few examples represent simple solutions to business problems—solutions that require nothing more than the use of free, unrestrained intelligence and imagination.

It is unfortunate that our business world has become so structured that it demands specialization to such a degree that young people feel the need to learn only specific trades. By getting that type of education they hope to be able to find their way into one of those corporate niches.

If we continue with the present trend of specialized education, we are going to be successful in keeping a steady supply of drones moving to a large beehive. Our country was not built by a bunch of drones. It was built by people.

Have we lost sight of the fact that people are the most important commodity we have? They are not a collection of drones. They are individuals—each with intelligence, imagination, curiosity, impulses, emotions, and ingenuity.

In my business I want people who have those intangible qualities. Anyone can meet them. They are marching across the pages of books—poetry, history, and novels.

My hope is that in the process of choosing a college to make your future fruitful, these thoughts will help you precipitate out the sludge and produce a clear, unmuddied solution. Good luck!

* The history and philosophy major did not go into the scrap-metal business. After a research sojourn in Colombia in which a town's history that he wrote became a television documentary, he is getting a Ph.D. in filmmaking at UCLA. But, Mr. Bittner reports, he's planning to make the scrap-metal company the subject of a film.

Index